Health and Safety

Knowledge and Skills for Social Care Workers series

The Knowledge and Skills for Social Care Workers series features accessible open learning workbooks which tackle a range of key subjects relevant to people working with adults in residential or domiciliary settings. Not just a source of guidance, these workbooks are also designed to meet the requirements of Health and Social Care (Adults) NVQ Level 3, with interactive exercises to develop practice.

other books in the series

Effective Communication
A Workbook for Social Care Workers
Suzan Collins
ISBN 978 1 84310 927 3

Safeguarding Adults
A Workbook for Social Care Workers
Suzan Collins
ISBN 978 1 84310 928 0

Reflecting On and Developing Your Practice
A Workbook for Social Care Workers
Suzan Collins
ISBN 978 1 84310 930 3

Health and Safety

A Workbook for Social Care Workers

Suzan Collins

Jessica Kingsley Publishers
London and Philadelphia

First published in 2009
by Jessica Kingsley Publishers
116 Pentonville Road
London N1 9JB, UK
and
400 Market Street, Suite 400
Philadelphia, PA 19106, USA

www.jkp.com

Copyright © Suzan Collins 2009

Library of Congress Cataloging in Publication Data
A CIP catalog record for this book is available from the Library of Congress

British Library Cataloguing in Publication Data
A CIP catalogue record for this book is available from the British Library

ISBN 978 1 84310 929 7

Printed and bound in Great Britain by
Athenaeum Press, Gateshead, Tyne and Wear

Acknowledgements

Shonagh Methven (Senior Business Partner (Health and Safety), United Response) for health and safety forms and for researching the definitions for 'accident, incident and near miss': www.unitedresponse.org.uk

Paul Hosking (Managing Director, AID Training and Operations Ltd) for photographs of health emergencies (i.e. signs of breathing, open the airways and rescue breaths), and fire extinguishers and for information on fire extinguishers and their purpose: www.aid-training.co.uk

Paul Tack (Health and Safety Manager, Livability) for information on disease and infection: www.livability.org.uk

Karen Nussey (Care Manager) for allowing me to photograph her hands to show the six steps to hand-washing.

Roy Prewer (Lowestoft Fire Oulton Broad, Suffolk) for photographs of fire extinguishers.

Simon Kent (Social Worker BA honours) for his advice and support.

Ben Horne (Lowestoft Fire and Rescue) for his support.

This workbook meets the requirements of the following standards, guidance and qualifications

Care Quality Commission (CQC)
Care Home for Adults Standard 35
Domiciliary Care Standard 19
General Social Care Council (GSCC)
Code of Practice Standards 3 and 4
Learning Disability Qualification Induction Award
LDQIA Level 3, Unit 303
National Vocational Qualification in Health and Social Care
NVQ HSC Level 3, Unit 32
Skills for Care (SfC)
Common Induction Standard 3

Contents

Introduction

As a social care worker you have a responsibility to contribute to a clean, safe and secure working environment for the people you support, yourself and others, for example colleagues and visitors. Depending on where you work you will also have a responsibility to support the people who use the service to contribute to a clean, safe and secure working environment.

This workbook will provide you with the knowledge to do this and covers the legislation of the Health and Safety at Work Act 1974 (HASAWA), which includes the Control of Substances Hazardous to Health 2002 (COSHH), Manual Handling Regulations 1992 (amended 2002), Lifting Operations and Lifting Equipment Regulations 1998 (LOLER), Provision and Use of Work Equipment Regulations 1998 (PUWER), Reporting of Injuries, Diseases and Dangerous Occurrences Regulations 1995 (RIDDOR), Health and Safety First Aid Regulations 1981, Health and Safety (Display Screen Equipment) Regulations 1992 (amended 2002), Electricity at Work Regulations 1989 and Personal Protective Equipment.

You will learn about what you can do to keep the workplace clean and free from germs, which also includes how to deal with hazardous waste. You will learn about your responsibilities and those of your employers. In addition you will learn about safe handling, medication, environmental hazards and how to promote choice and empower the people who live in the service (workplace). This can involve risk taking, therefore part of your role may involve assessing and managing risks. You will also learn what to do in an emergency such as a water or gas leak, fire, health emergency, intruder and so on.

It is not always possible for staff to be taken off the rota to attend a training course and so this training workbook has been devised. It uses a variety of training methods:

- reading passages where you will expand your knowledge

- completing exercises

- completing a self-assessment tool which shows you the knowledge you now have.

As a social care worker, you have to work to certain standards, which are set out by various professional bodies. This workbook links to several standards and if you are not familiar with them, here is a brief explanation of each one.

Learning Disability Qualification Induction Award (LDQ IA) is an induction award that all new staff working with people with learning disabilities must complete within three months of being in post. This workbook meets the communication requirements of the Level 3 award, Unit 303.

Skills for Care (SfC) has a set of standards called Common Induction Standards and all new staff in the care sector (except those who are supporting people with learning disabilities) have to complete these with their manager within three months of being in post. This workbook meets the requirements of Standard 3.

Care Quality Commission (CQC) took over the work of the Commission for Social Care Inspection (CSCI) on 1 April 2009 (it also took over the work of the Healthcare Commission and the Mental Health Act Commission). The CQC has sets of standards for you and your workplace to meet. There are different sets of standards and it will depend on where you work as to which standards you need to work to. If you are unsure please ask your manager. This workbook meets the requirements of Care Homes for Adults Standard 35 (Department of Health 2003) and Domiciliary Care Standard 19 (Department of Health 2000) as follows:

- Care Homes for Adults Standard 35 (35.3): Training in safe work practices within six months of being in post.

- Domiciliary Care Standard 19 (19.5): Required training on health and safety.

General Social Care Council (GSCC) has a Code of Practice with six standards, which reflect professional conduct and practice that is required by you and your employer. This workbook meets the requirements of Standards 3 and 4 (please see pp.16–18 for more details).

NVQ HSC is a *National Vocational Qualification in Health and Social Care.*

Towards the end of the workbook you will be asked to complete a self-assessment tool on what you have learnt from completing this workbook. Once you have completed this, your manager or trainer will complete the certificate and give it to you.

This workbook has been written first and foremost to enable you to ensure that the people you support are in a safe and secure environment and to enable you to complete health and safety training, without leaving the workplace.

If you are thinking about doing or working towards an NVQ Level 3 in Health and Social Care, you will find that this workbook is a great help to you.

The Health and Social Care Level 3 has four core units and four optional units. This workbook is one of the four core units written to show the knowledge specification. The other three core units are available in this series of books: *Safeguarding Adults, Reflecting on and Developing Your Practice* and *Effective Communication.*

When you have registered for an NVQ, you will be allocated an NVQ Assessor who will arrange to observe you in the workplace and guide you through your NVQ award. This guidance will involve devising action plans, which will consist of things like:

- Writing an account of how you did something in the workplace, e.g. helping someone to make a cup of tea, or providing support to enable a service user to follow a training programme, identifying risks, supporting someone to go to the shops, etc. This is called a 'self-reflective account' (SRA).

- Asking others to write an account of what you have done. This is called a 'witness report' (WR).

- Completing a set of questions which is called 'the knowledge specification'. This is where you can use this workbook for reference.

This workbook covers all the knowledge specification requirements for the NVQ Unit 32, 'Promote, monitor and maintain health, safety and security in the working environment', which can be found towards the end of this workbook (see Knowledge Specification Chart).

I hope that you find this a useful workbook and wish you well in your career. This workbook can be:

- read straight through from front to back

- read from front to back, answering the questions as you go, and these can be used as evidence towards the NVQ Unit 32

- used as a reference book.

In this workbook I have referred to the people you support as 'individuals', 'service users' or 'he/him', rather than continually writing he/she, him/her.

Name of Learner: . . . .

Signature of Learner:. . . . . Date: . . . . :

Name of Manager or Trainer: . . . .

Signature of Manager or Trainer: . . . . Date: . . . .

Workplace address or name of organization:

. . . .

. . . .

. . . .

Health and Safety Policy and Legislation

HEALTH AND SAFETY POLICY

If your place of work has five or more employees, there must be a written health and safety policy which should contain information on:

- the name of the person implementing the policy and the names of others who have responsibility for specific health and safety hazards

- safe methods for handling

- identifying hazards and how to deal with them

- how to evacuate the building in case of a fire, gas leak, or other emergency

- how to record accidents at work (some places of work have an accident book; others have accident forms)

- suitable training and supervision for employees.

How to encourage staff to follow health and safety policy

All staff must follow health and safety practices. If you find that other members of staff are not following health and safety practices, you could try the following:

- act as a good role model for them to emulate

- politely bring to their attention that if they did the task a different way, they would be meeting health and safety requirements.

LEGISLATION

In addition to your work's health and safety policy, you will need to know about relevant legislation in order to create a safe and secure working environment. The main piece of legislation that applies to your work setting is the Health and Safety at Work Act 1974. This HASAWA is the law and the regulations below are implemented under it.

Regulations made under the Health and Safety at Work Act which are applicable to the care sector are:

- Control of Substances Hazardous to Health 2002 (COSHH)

- Manual Handling Regulations 1992 (amended 2002)
- Lifting Operations and Lifting Equipment Regulations 1998 (LOLER)
- Provision and Use of Work Equipment Regulations 1998 (PUWER)
- Reporting of Injuries, Diseases and Dangerous Occurrences Regulations 1995 (RIDDOR)
- Health and Safety First Aid Regulations 1981
- Health and Safety (Display Screen Equipment) Regulations 1992 (amended 2002)
- Electricity at Work Regulations 1989
- Personal Protective Equipment 1992.

All these regulations are linked to people's health and safety as identified by the Health and Safety Executive (HSE).

> Our mission is to protect people's health and safety by ensuring that risks in the changing work place are properly controlled. (Health and Safety Commission 2008)

You need to know:

- where you can find out more about these regulations
- where your organization's policies and procedures are
- what your responsibilities are, and those of your employers and of the people you support.

Responsibilities for Health and Safety

EMPLOYERS' RESPONSIBILITIES

Your employer has responsibilities for:

- ensuring compliance with relevant legislation

- providing a workplace that is safe

- ensuring that equipment is checked regularly

- ensuring that policies and procedures are in place and staff are familiar with them

- providing information on health and safety

- assessing and reducing risks

- monitoring staff performance

- ensuring staff are trained to do their job

- ensuring equipment is available if needed and in good condition

- putting policies and procedures in place and ensuring staff are familiar with them

- following Standards 2 and 3 of the General Social Care Council, which follow.

RESPONSIBILITIES ACCORDING TO THE GENERAL SOCIAL CARE COUNCIL CODE OF PRACTICE

GSCC Standard 2

As a social care employer, you must have written policies and procedures in place to enable social care workers to meet the GSCC's Code of Practice for Social Care Workers.
This includes:

- Implementing and monitoring written policies on: confidentiality; equal opportunities; risk assessment.

substance abuse; record keeping; and the acceptance of money or personal gifts from service users or carers.

- Effectively managing and supervising staff to support effective practice and good conduct and supporting staff to address deficiencies in their performance.

- Having systems in place to enable social care workers to report inadequate resources or operational difficulties which might impede the delivery of safe care and working with them and relevant authorities to address those issue.

- Supporting social care workers to meet the GSCC's Code of Practice for Social Care Workers and not requiring them to do anything that would put their compliance with that code at risk. (General Social Care Council 2002)

GSCC Standard 3

As a social care employer, you must provide training and development opportunities to enable social care workers to strengthen and develop their skills and knowledge.

This includes:

- Providing induction, training and development opportunities to help social care workers do their jobs effectively and prepare for new and changing roles and responsibilities.

- Contributing to the provision of social care and social work education and training, including using effective workplace assessment and practice learning.

- Supporting staff in posts subject to registration to meet the GSCC's eligibility criteria for registration and its requirements for continuing professional development.

- Responding appropriately to social care workers who seek assistance because they do not feel able or adequately prepared to carry out any aspects of their work. (General Social Care Council 2002)

You have responsibilities for:

- attending training

- reading and following policies and procedures, including risk assessments

- using any equipment provided and putting it away afterwards

- taking care of the people you support and yourself

- cooperating with your employer on health and safety matters

- reporting any concerns you have, e.g. broken equipment and furniture, staff not following procedures

- maintaining a safe environment, e.g. keeping windows and doors locked

- following Standards 3 and 4 of the General Social Care Council.

GSCC Standard 3

As a social care worker, you must promote the independence of service users while protecting them as far as possible from harm.

This includes:

- Promoting the independence of service users and assisting them to understand and exercise their rights.

- Using established processes and procedures to challenge and report dangerous, abusive, discriminatory or exploitative behaviour and practice.

- Following practice and procedures designed to keep you and other people safe from violent and abusive behaviour at work.

- Bringing to the attention of your employer or the appropriate authority resource or operational difficulties that might get in the way of the delivery of safe care.

- Informing your employer or an appropriate authority where the practice of colleagues may be unsafe or adversely affecting the standards of care.

- Complying with employer's health and safety policies, including those relating to substance abuse.

- Helping service user and carers to make complaints, taking complaints seriously and responding to them or passing them to the appropriate person.

- Recognising and using responsibly the power that comes from your work with service users and carers. (General Social Care Council 2002)

GSCC Standard 4

As a social care worker, you must respect the rights of service users while seeking to ensure that their behaviour does not harm themselves or other people.

This includes:

- Recognising that service users have the right to take risks and helping them to identify and manage potential and actual risks to themselves or others.

- Following risk assessment policies and procedures to assess whether the behaviour of service users presents a risk of harm to themselves or others.

- Taking necessary steps to minimise the risks of service users from doing actual or potential harm to themselves or other people.

- Ensuring that relevant colleagues and agencies are informed about the outcomes and implications of risk assessments. (General Social Care Council 2002)

> You also have responsibility for the health and safety of yourself and others at work.

PERSONAL RESPONSIBILITIES

In addition to the GSCC Code of Practice responsibilities, you are responsible for the way you dress. For your own safety it is advisable that *you do not* wear the following to work:

- *Open-toed shoes* or shoes with raised heels as these will not give you any protection if someone accidentally steps on your toes or you drop something on them. Shoes with heels will not enable you to balance should you have to bend your knees to move an object or a person.

- *Tight clothing* as this will restrict your movement for lifting and/or when supporting people who present challenging behaviour; it is advisable to wear loose clothing. If you are supporting older people you will be required to wear a uniform which is likely to be a tunic with trousers. A pleat in the middle of the back will allow free movement, and will plenty of room around the shoulders.

- *Earrings* other than stud earrings, excessive jewellery around the neck and/or face jewellery as these can catch on things or the people you are supporting.

Another key responsibility for the individual is the responsibility for reporting and recording, which will be explored in greater detail in the next chapter.

RIGHTS AND RESPONSIBILITIES OF THE PEOPLE YOU SUPPORT

The people you support also have rights and responsibilities.

Service users' rights

Service users have the right to participate in meetings and to make decisions about their preferences and choices and when planning risk assessments. They also have the right to report or express any concerns they may have – whether about health and safety or not. Here are a few examples:

- neighbours throwing litter into the garden

- another service user entering their bedroom at night

- call buzzers being left ringing for a long time and causing distress

- not liking the way they are hoisted

- not liking the way they are fed – they may feel they are being rushed to eat their meal when they are a slow eater.

 One of your responsibilities from the GSCC Code of Practice is to help the people you support to make complaints, take the complaints seriously and respond to the complaints or pass them to the appropriate person.

Do you know how to respond to a complaint?	Yes/No
Do you know who to pass the complaint on to?	Yes/No
Do the people you support know that they can comment and raise concerns?	Yes/No
Is your comments and complaints procedure available for the service users to read?	Yes/No
Is a comments and complaints book or form to record comments or complaints available for you to see?	Yes/No
Is your comments and complaints procedure available in different languages, or in images for those who are unable to read?	Yes/No

✍ If you have answered 'No' to any of these, what might you do about it?

. . . .

. . . .

. . . .

Service users' responsibilities

Service users have the following responsibilities in relation to health and safety:

- to smoke only in the designated area

- to follow policies and procedures

- to keep windows and doors locked at night and when leaving their room or going out

- to keep the areas they use and their own bedrooms tidy.

The level of responsibility the service users have will depend on their ability to understand the consequences of not carrying out their responsibilities.

Recording and Reporting

THE IMPORTANCE OF RECORDING AND REPORTING

Both you and your manager have responsibilities for reporting and recording significant events: either when something has happened which should not have happened, or when something has not happened as it is supposed to.

It is very important that things are recorded and reported as this enables your manager and others to review procedures and prevent unwanted things from happening again – for example, if someone has tripped on a frayed carpet, reporting and recording the event will make it likely that the carpet is fixed and a future accident avoided.

Another reason to record it is to provide proof that you have acted correctly and told someone about an incident or accident. This can be important if in future someone questions why something was not flagged as a problem.

For each event to be recorded or reported, there is an appropriate place to record or report it.

For example, if you supported Mr X with his personal care you would record this in his care plan. If Mrs Y's care plan says that she washes independently but she had a fall and may need assistance, you would record this in her care plan and complete an accident form/incident book. This can be written in a care plan. If the milkman did not call on Saturday as he usually does, and so he has not been paid and the money is left in the safe, this should be written in the staff communication book.

RECORDING HEALTH AND SAFETY ISSUES

Health and safety issues should be recorded:

- on an incident or accident form (see pp.26–27)

- on a Regulation 37 form and sent to CSCI

- in the service user's file.

It is very important that all reports are passed on to the relevant department, e.g. Health and Safety Executive, local authority or the Environmental Health Department.

Your organization will have its own policy informing you on which forms should be used for which health and safety issue, e.g. something like a small paper cut *may* only be recorded in the service user's file and other accidents etc., such as a broken limb, will be recorded on all three forms. Please check with your manager what the procedure is in your workplace.

As mentioned near to the start of this workbook there are some CSCI standards that staff need to follow and in with these standards are some regulations. One of these regulations is called 'Regulation 37' and this requires that CSCI are informed of any event which adversely affects the well-being or safety of a service user. Here are some examples:

- the conviction of a registered person (this could be the manager or owner of the care home)

- an allegation or instance of abuse, neglect or other harm that has been reported to the police

- threatening or challenging behaviour by one service user towards another

- threatening or challenging behaviour by a service user towards staff

- staff levels falling below the minimum level agreed with the CSCI

- missing service user

- error in administering medication to a service user

- the death of any person who uses the service, the outbreak of any infectious disease, a serious injury to a service user or any theft, burglary or accident in a care home or Adult Placement carer's home

- any allegation of misconduct by the registered person or any person who works at the care home

- any incident reported to or investigated by the police

- any absence of a registered person for 28 or more days.

It will depend on which service you work in, such as a care home or person's own home, as to the timescale of when you need to notify CSCI because the standards are different for each of these two settings. More information about this and an example of a Regulation 37 form which can be used can be found on the CQC website: http://www.cqc.org.uk/guidanceforprofessionals/socialcare/careproviders/guidance.cfm?widCall1=customWidgets.content_view_1&cit_id=2525

✎ Please ask your manager where the incident or accident forms or book are kept and also who has the responsibility to inform CSCI via the Regulation 37 form.

. . . .

. . . .

. . . .

. . . .

WHEN AND HOW TO REPORT

When and how the reporting and recording are completed is to an extent at the discretion of your manager. For example, if you are completing the care plan, you will complete it either during or at the end of your time spent supporting the service user. You will inform the service user what you are going to do and where possible you can ask the service user what he or she wishes for you to write. Other times you will do this as soon as you can, for example if there has been an accident, incident or near miss – more on these below.

If you are on duty when an accident or incident has happened, you will be very busy dealing with this and also supporting those who have been affected by the accident or illness. You may feel that the last thing you want to do is complete an accident or incident form. However, remember that *it is a legal requirement* to record and report accidents, incidents and near misses and you must do this at the earliest opportunity. If your manager is not in the building and you cannot contact him or her, you must inform the manager on call if you have one. More on this below.

THE DIFFERENCE BETWEEN 'ACCIDENTS', 'INCIDENTS' AND 'NEAR MISSES'

- *Accident*: an undesired set of circumstances which give rise to ill health, injury, damage, production losses or increased liabilities.

- *Incident*: any undesired circumstance or 'near miss' which could cause accidents.

- *Near miss*: an accident event which does not realize its potential for injury or damage. (Health and Safety Executive 1997)

Records need to be kept on all accidents, incidents and near misses. Some organizations use an accident book and/or incident book while others use accident and incident forms which are on a triplicate pad.

On a triplicate pad, you write on the top page and a copy of what you write will be left on the two pages below it. The three sheets are usually different colours, and each will go to a different person after your manager has signed it – usually, one is kept on file in the workplace, one is sent to the health and safety manager and one is sent to the area manager.

This workbook features samples of different forms that you may come across in your workplace on the following pages:

- Accident, Incident, Near Miss on pp.26–27.

- Risk Assessment on pp.40–42.

- Control of Substances Hazardous to Health (COSHH) on p.48.

- ABC (Antecedent, Behaviour, Consequences) chart on p.105.

THE DIFFERENCE BETWEEN 'MINOR' AND 'MAJOR' ACCIDENTS

While any accident is undesirable, they are usually classified in two ways: minor and major:

- *Minor accident*: paper cut on finger.

- *Major accident*: broken arm or leg.

Ask your manager if you would record both of the above accidents on the accident or incident form or just the major accident, and record the paper cut in the service user's file.

. . . .

. . . .

. . . .

. . . .

DISEASES, INJURIES AND DANGEROUS OCCURRENCES

Your manager has a legal requirement to report notifiable diseases, injuries and dangerous occurrences to the relevant enforcing authority in accordance with the regulations of RIDDOR (Reporting of Injuries, Diseases and Dangerous Occurrence Regulations 1995).

Injuries, diseases and dangerous occurrences need to be reported, and your organization's policy will tell you who these need to be reported to. The policy will also tell you that the manager has the responsibility to do the reporting and that the following need to be reported:

- someone needing to take three or more days off work after an accident

- disease (including poisoning)

- major injury

- work-related death

- dangerous occurrence (near miss).

THINGS TO REMEMBER WHEN RECORDING AND REPORTING

When filling in any kind of report, remember that all entries must be:

- *Written in black ink*: if you make an error do not use whiting-out or correction fluid. Instead, put a line through the error, initial it and carry on writing.

- *Signed and dated*: this a legal requirement and is useful if you need to check when it happened. The signature means that the person signing the form is confirming that what he or she has written is a correct account of what happened.

Fact versus opinion

When recording or reporting, you must ensure that you keep to factual information: what actually happened. If a report includes opinions, it must be made clear that these are only opinions and not factual statements. An opinion is a person's version of what he or she thinks happened or assumes to be true.

> A fact: It is raining today.
>
> An opinion: I think it might rain today.

Data protection

The recording of an incident or accident must contain what happened but must not show personal details of the people involved unless consent has been given – this is due to the legal requirements of the Data Protection Act 1998.

The Act will be reflected in your organization's policies and procedures and is in place to protect the rights of the individual. It affects:

- access to information about people, as individuals can ask to see information written about them

- how long information is kept on the individual

- what information is kept on the individual

- how the information is held

- how it will be disposed of.

You will be privy to sensitive and personal information and, where possible, you must get the individual's permission for information to be used where it is helpful to provide care and support. When the individual is first registered with you s/he will be asked to complete forms and on one of these forms will be a question asking if the information given on these forms can be shared with others who need to know in order to provide a consistent approach of care and support. The consent form can then be placed on the individual's file.

For example:

- Mrs Y has a sensitive bladder and is unable to take herself to the toilet.

- Mrs Z is unable to communicate verbally and finds this very frustrating; sometimes this results in her hitting others.

- Mr X has schizophrenia and the medication he takes controls it; however, there are a few rare occasions when he forgets to take it and he becomes unwell. Mr X has told you that when this happens he wants you to provide care and support but in a different way, e.g. if the care plan says you will support him with his weekly shopping on a Thursday when he is well the care plan for 'less well days' may be that you get the shopping for him, or he may want less support, or support from those closest to him.

SAMPLE ACCIDENT/INCIDENT REPORT FORM

Area		Date	
Service			
Type of report	☐ Accident ☐ Incident ☐ Near miss	Duration	

WHO WAS INVOLVED? (indicate who was injured by writing after their name)		
Client	Staff (name and job title)	Other people (witnesses)

WHAT HAPPENED?

- ☐ Verbal and physical aggression
- ☐ Illness/seizure
- ☐ Trip/fall/minor injury
- ☐ Money error
- ☐ Road accident
- ☐ Ingestion of harmful substance
- ☐ Water/gas/electric fault
- ☐ Physical aggression

- ☐ Verbal aggression
- ☐ Racial/sexual harassment
- ☐ Inappropriate behaviour
- ☐ Theft
- ☐ Fire alarm activated
- ☐ Missing person
- ☐ Choking
- ☐ Complaint

- ☐ Self injury
- ☐ Unexplained injury
- ☐ Equipment fault
- ☐ Fire
- ☐ Drug refusal
- ☐ Drug overdose
- ☐ Drug error
- ☐ Other_____

OUTCOMES	
Injury	Give details of any property damaged
☐ None ☐ Minor ☐ Serious ☐ Major Description of injury to the person we support, member of staff or other people ☐ Bite ☐ Cut/scratch ☐ Bruise ☐ Scald/burn ☐ Break ☐ Internal ☐ Strain ☐ Stress ☐ Sharps ☐ Shock ☐ Other If injury: ☐ Notifiable ☐ Medical advice sought	

ANY OTHER FACTS

Signature of person completing form. Date. . . . .

Signature of line manager. . . . . Date. . . . .

Signature of area/regional manager. Date. . . . .

Monitoring the Workplace for Health and Safety

It is important to maintain a healthy, clean, safe environment. This chapter outlines the measures in place to check that a workplace meets the required standards and also how you can help to ensure that health and safety requirements are met by monitoring the workplace.

COMMISSION FOR SOCIAL CARE INSPECTION AND REGULATION 26 AUDITS

The Commission for Social Care Inspection has standards and regulations that need to be followed: in particular Regulation 26, which is where your manager's employer visits the workplace once a month unannounced, carries out a Regulation 26 audit, and records that the audit has taken place. The purpose of the audit is to monitor the conduct of the care home. The audit is often referred to by managers as a 'Reg 26' and is completed by an off-site manager who is not part of the immediate team to ensure that it is carried out in an objective way. (In domiciliary care settings, under Domiciliary Care Standards Regulation 21, the registered person will evaluate the quality of the services.)

In more detail, the purpose of this audit is to:

- speak with the people who use the service and staff (individually and together)

- inspect the premises

- note standards of care

- check concerns and/or complaints

- check staffing levels

- check any health and safety concerns

- check team meetings

- check supervision, including training needs and the percentage of staff who have an NVQ

- check people's support plans

- check that actions from the previous Reg 26 visit have been carried out.

The Commission for Social Care Inspection will also carry out unannounced audits and will cover the areas above and probably more. These are called 'unannounced inspections' and the frequency of these inspections will depend on how well your organization meets the standards. Individual residential services are graded:

- 3 stars – excellent
- 2 stars – good
- 1 star – adequate
- 0 star – poor
- not yet rated
- suspended rating.

ENSURING THAT HEALTH AND SAFETY STANDARDS ARE MET

In order to ensure a safe and healthy workplace, you need to make sure not only that you follow systems that are in place, but also that you are vigilant to any health and safety issues that come up throughout the course of your daily work.

Monthly checks on equipment

It is the responsibility of all employees to monitor and maintain any equipment in the workplace. One way of ensuring this is done would be to designate one person with health and safety responsibility to carry out a detailed regular health and safety check. This would usually be done on a monthly basis and would involve the use of a checklist of health and safety issues for the whole building. Examples of items on the checklist will be to ascertain if regular checks or tests have been done on, for example:

- temperatures of fridge, freezer and water
- fire drills
- fire alarms
- gas boilers or gas fires (should be checked annually)
- electrical items (these require Portable Appliance Testing, or 'PAT', carried out by a qualified electrician, who places a dated sticker on each item to show when it next requires a PAT)
- curtains, bedding and furniture – that all are fire retardant.

Daily monitoring of hazards and risks

You should automatically check for hazards or risks when you are on shift. This may be a very informal process of being aware and looking around you, but it is just as important as formal monthly checks.

While reading through this workbook you will come across the words 'hazards' and 'risks'. Here is a brief explanation of what they are and how they differ.

A *hazard* is anything that could cause harm. For example:

Hazard	The harm it could do
Knife	Cut
Electricity	Electrocution
Wet floor	Slips, trips and falls

A *risk* is the likelihood that someone or something could be harmed. For example, a staff member's mobile phone being left on will increase the risk of him or her making a mistake when distracted by a call or text. Many organizations have a policy to say that personal mobiles should be turned off while you are at work.

Hazards in the workplace

 Below is a list of examples of hazards in the workplace which you should look out for, along with a recommended plan of action. Read through them and tick any that you have seen happen in your workplace.

Workplace hazard	Action required	Have you seen this happen?
Hot water temperature	Risk of scalding. In residential settings, water temperatures should be tested regularly. Water is stored at a temperature of at least 60°C and distributed at 50°C minimum, to prevent risks from Legionella. To prevent risks from scalding, pre-set valves of a type unaffected by changes in water pressure and which have fail safe devices are fitted locally to provide water close to 43°C. (CSCI Standard 25 Older People Standards)	

Workplace hazard	Action required	Have you seen this happen?
Radiators hot to touch	Risk of burning if someone leans against or falls on a hot radiator. The heating should have a thermostat that can be adjusted. Radiator guards can also be purchased.	
Chemicals in unlabelled containers	Risk of poisoning, chemical burn or skin irritation. If there is no label the contents cannot be identified and should not be used. If an individual is burned or drinks some of it, you will not know what was in the unlabelled container to provide the appropriate treatment. Dispose of any unlabelled chemicals appropriately.	
Air freshener or body spray	Risk of burning and explosion if sprayed near naked flames. Excessive use can cause people to cough and experience breathing difficulties and potentially cause harm to the chest.	
Windows that open widely	Risk of individuals falling out of the window. Windows should be modified to prevent this happening, e.g. have a catch to restrict how far they can open.	
Wheelchair in the middle of a room, hall or corridor	Risk of individuals bumping into it or falling. Move to a safer place to prevent this.	
Trailing leads from a TV or DVD player	Risk of tripping and falling. Use cable clips or cable ties to keep them together and out of the way.	
Broken lock on a door or window	Potential for an intruder to enter the building or for a service user to exit the building. Also a risk for a person to fall out of an unlocked window. Ensure all locks are made secure.	
Items left on the stairs	Items left on stairs can cause people to trip over them or try to avoid them and lose their footing. Remove them and place them somewhere safe.	
Stairways not fitted with handrails	Risk of falling: if there is not a handrail you will need to walk with the service user to ensure he or she uses the stairs safely and if possible arrange for a handrail to be fitted.	

Workplace hazard	Action required	Have you seen this happen?
Poor lighting	Risk of falling and injury, particularly if stairs are poorly lit and for those with poor sight or who are not very mobile. Poor lighting can also cause headaches, fatigue and eye strain, as well as hindering communication if someone cannot clearly see your facial expressions when you talk. Introduce good lighting and in the mean time walk with the service user to ensure he is able to travel safely.	
Poor ventilation	Risk of tiredness and stress – introduce better quality ventilation.	
A light bulb with the wrong wattage for a lampshade	If a light bulb is too hot, it will scorch the lampshade and pose the risk of a fire. Unplug the lamp, ensure the light bulb is cool, remove it and replace with a bulb of the appropriate wattage (the lampshade should specify).	
Uneven floors	Risk of slipping, tripping and falling. Put a sign up to prevent people walking on the floor and ideally replace the floor.	
Cold environment	A cold setting can cause parts of the body such as the fingers to stiffen and increase the risk of things being dropped – for example, someone may spill a hot cup of tea into his lap. Also, stiffening of the joints increases the risk of falls.	
Wet floors	Risk of slipping. A sign should be displayed clearly stating (and showing with a picture) that the floor is wet and could be slippery.	
Polished floors	Risk of slipping, particularly if the people you support walk around in socks. Advise individuals to wear slippers, but bear in mind it is their choice. If they prefer to wear socks, they may wish to purchase socks with a tread that grips to reduce the risk of slipping.	
Loose mats or rugs	Risk of slipping and tripping, especially if the rug is on a slippery floor. To prevent injury you could use a non-slip mat under the rug or use a multi-grip backing to stop it slipping.	

Workplace hazard	Action required	Have you seen this happen?
Frayed or worn carpets	Risk of slipping, tripping and falling. If it is a rug, remove it. If not, put a sign up to prevent people walking on the section of carpet. Worn carpets are also very hard to clean and vacuum.	
Items stacked high	Whether paperwork or filing, pads, towels or sheets, if they are stacked high and not at eye level, you will have to reach for them, with a risk that they could topple over and cause injury.	
Unguarded fire	Risk that hot coals could fall out onto the carpet and cause a fire, injury and damage. Risk that sparks can jump out and cause injury or fire. Ensure a guard is put in place and report it immediately.	
Fire doors wedged open	Fire doors must not be wedged open. If they are wedged open they will not prevent the spread of a fire and will not block the flow of air. These doors should not be open unless held open by a magnet which releases once a fire alarm goes off. If wedged open, you should close them immediately.	
Fire exits blocked	If the exits are blocked you will not be able to get out if there is a fire. Exits should be clear at all times. If they are blocked you need to unblock them immediately.	
Stacks of old newspapers piled in a corner	Remove immediately as this could help a fire to spread. Place them in the recycling bin or ask one of the people you support to accompany you to the recycling depot. Encourage them to regularly put the papers into the recycling bin.	
Overloaded electric sockets	Sockets should not be overloaded as this can cause a fire. You can purchase a multiway adapter with a surge protector which will have many sockets on it. If the socket is overloaded you need to unplug the sockets.	
Picture frames with glass in them	These can be hazardous if you are supporting people who present challenging behaviour as the frames could be thrown. You could secure the glass with adhesive tape or remove the glass completely. Please discuss with the people you support before altering their picture frames.	

Workplace hazard	Action required	Have you seen this happen?
In the kitchen		
Toasted bread does not pop up in the toaster	The people you support may be tempted to put a knife in the toaster to get the toasted bread out and they could be electrocuted. You should unplug the toaster, turn it upside down and shake it.	
A toaster with sides that become hot	Poses the risk of burning. Ideally, replace the toaster. If this is not possible, a solution could be to risk assess the equipment and, if appropriate, put a note by the toaster stating that the sides of the toaster become hot when in use (with an appropriate symbol).	
In the bathroom		
Bleach bottle left in toilet	Risk of poisoning and skin irritation. Individuals could accidentally drink it. Keep in a secure and safe place.	
In the garden		
Wasps	Risk of stinging and an allergic reaction. Some individuals who get stung could have an anaphylactic shock and require immediate emergency treatment. If this is the case they will have been prescribed emergency medication. As a preventative measure everyone could use a repellent spray when they are outside.	
An electric lawn mower without a circuit breaker	Risk of injury. A circuit breaker (safety RLD adaptor) should be plugged into the electrical point in the garden and the plug of the mower plugged into the adapter. This adapter will cut off the electricity if any problems arise.	
Slippery garden paths	Risk of slipping and falling. Why is it slippery? Is it because of wet leaves or moss growing on the path? If so, sweep up the leaves and clean the path. This hazard should be on the risk assessment for the garden.	
Bushes blocking the path	Individuals can walk into the bushes and become unsteady or catch their clothes on them. Bushes should be trimmed back regularly and form part of the risk assessment for the garden.	

Workplace hazard	Action required	Have you seen this happen?
Uneven path	People can slip, trip or fall if the path is uneven. Where possible put a sign up and put something over the uneven piece, like a chair. If all of the path is dangerous, the chair should be used to block the path.	
Wheelbarrow with punctured tyre	This can cause a back injury and/or the wheelbarrow to turn over onto its side, spilling its contents. This must be taken out of circulation immediately and a notice put on it to say what is wrong with it and 'do not use'.	
Unstable table umbrella	This could collapse on a service user or the service user could injure himself by trying to put it back up. Look at why the umbrella is unstable: is it because it was not put up correctly? If you are unable to make it stable, put it in a place away from the people you support with a note on it saying that it should not be used and why.	
Unsteady chair	Risk of falling. Look at why the chair is unstable: is the chair old and weak or placed on an uneven surface? Would different style chairs be better? If you cannot make it stable, place the chair in a place away from the people you support with a note on it saying that it should not be used and why.	

Remember to *record and report* any hazard you see! If you do this, the people you support will benefit from a *hazard-free environment*.

✍ If you have ticked any of the above, please write down what action you intend to take.

. . . .

. . . .

. . . .

. . . .

. . . .

. . . .

Risk Assessments

THE IMPORTANCE OF RISK ASSESSMENTS

The Management of Health and Safety at Work Regulations 1992 require risks to be assessed in all areas of your work. Risks to the people you support, yourself and other people must be assessed. Your organization has a legal obligation to ensure the health and safety of the people you support and staff by identifying hazards and putting control measures in place to reduce risks.

Risks must be recorded on a risk assessment form in areas where people are especially vulnerable (you can see a sample risk assessment form on pp.40–42). In homes it may be necessary to have formal risk assessments in place around particular areas of work, including bathing, behaviour, mental health needs, challenging behaviour, working alone, working in the kitchen, manual handling, working with computers and working while pregnant.

A decision about whether to allow a risk is balanced against the benefits of allowing it to be taken. There are risks attached to almost everything we do: crossing the road, going to a night club, getting a bus, going to the bank, having friends, being in a relationship. If we did not take risks, we would not learn and develop and our opportunities in life would be limited. Your role is to enable the people you support to understand the risks associated with making choices. This does not mean that if there is a risk then the choice does not happen.

THE POSITIVE SIDE OF RISK: SERVICE USERS MAKING CHOICES

We all need activities and goals in our lives and this is no different for the people you support. Within your role as a social care worker, you will need to know how to support service users to make choices and decisions, identify activities and goals, and play a role in enabling the service users to achieve them. Some service users will achieve them without your help. It will depend on the individual as to how much support the service user would like or may need.

Each service user will have a support plan which is tailored to their needs. It will have detailed information on what the service user would like to do or achieve and how the support must be provided and by whom, such as yourself, advocate, social services etc. The location of the support plans could be in different places depending on where you work. If you work in a residential setting they will be in a locked cabinet and the service user will have his or her own copy but if service users live in their own home then they will keep it where they want to keep it. It is important that you record in it after you have supported the service user.

As mentioned earlier, some information that you read when considering the potential risk to a service user will be found in care plans and risk assessments where appropriate, and may be sensitive and confidential. You are being trusted not to tell other people unless there is a reason to do so and with the individual's consent. Once the individual has given permission for information to be used to provide care and support, he or she does not need to be asked again, although you may like to ask the service user from time to time to ensure he or she still agrees to it.

Everyone has the right to choose what they want to do, where they go, what they wear, and so on, and they may be able to make these choices independently. Others may require some help, which can be offered by verbally discussing ideas or using different methods of communication (you can find out more about these methods in another workbook in this series, *Effective Communication*).

Some of the people you support may be able to make choices, others may not. It is wrong to assume that if someone has dementia, for example, he cannot make any kind of choice. The key issue is whether he is able to understand the risks attached to his choices.

MAKING CHOICES: THE MENTAL CAPACITY ACT 2005

For guidance on mental capacity, you should refer to the Mental Capacity Act 2005. This Act provides a framework to protect the people you support in decision making.

You may have a copy of this Act in your workplace; if not you will be able to view a copy on the Internet and you will find the web address on p.125. It has pages of information on how to ascertain if the people you support can make decisions. Please have a look at a copy, in particular sections on:

- five key principles

- independent mental capacity advocate (IMCA)

- the making of 'living wills'

- the new criminal offence of ill treatment or neglect.

MAKING A DECISION THAT INVOLVES A RISK

If the service user makes a choice that presents a risk, you can have a meeting to discuss this with him and also your manager. Both may wish to invite others along to discuss it too – perhaps a relative, social worker or advocate. The meeting can assess the likelihood of the risk, who might be at risk and ways to reduce these risks. All of this will be recorded on a risk assessment form.

As a social care worker you have a responsibility to protect the people you support, to think about the risks in a service user's life and how to reduce these risks. By identifying the risks early on you will go a long way in protecting the service user from harm and/or abuse.

In the past service users have been prevented from doing things that benefit them because of the potential risks attached to them. Some staff think that a risk assessment stops an activity happening but this is not what a risk assessment should be about.

> A risk assessment should be seen as a tool to **enable** experience rather than **prevent** an activity.

When completing a risk assessment, questions are asked about hazards and, by identifying them, it enables potential risks to be discussed and control measures to be put in place to reduce them.

There will be times when the people you support want to do something and a hazard could be attached to it. Here are some examples of what the people you support may like to do:

- make themselves a cup of tea

- learn how to cook beans on toast

- go to the shops by themselves

- travel on a bus or train by themselves

- clean their own bedroom

- have a sexual relationship.

> Under the Management of Health and Safety at Work Regulations 1999 risks in the workplace must be assessed. Once the risk is identified, measures need to be in place to reduce these risks.

RISK ASSESSMENT COVER SHEET

HAZARD BEING ASSESSED:. . . . .

This form should be completed when staff have read and understood a new risk assessment or when one has been updated.

SERVICE:. . . . . DATE OF ASSESSMENT:. . . . .

PREPARED BY:. . . . . READ and AGREED BY: . . . .

Name	Date	Signature

HAZARD BEING ASSESSED:. . . . .

NAME OF SERVICE	ADDRESS	DATE OF ASSESSMENT	ASSESSMENT PREPARED BY

HAZARD	WHO MIGHT BE HARMED?	WOULD ANY PROPERTY BE AFFECTED?
Describe the hazard that you might expect to result in significant harm under the conditions at this location.	List staff, service users and other visitors to the premises who may be affected. Be specific.	Describe any potential damage to building or other items of property.
IS THE RISK ADEQUATELY CONTROLLED?	**WHAT FURTHER ACTION IS NECESSARY TO CONTROL THE RISK?**	**WHEN WILL THIS ASSESSMENT BE REVIEWED?**
List all the precautions that already exist, e.g. have you provided adequate information and/or training? • Do the precautions meet any legal requirements? • represent good practice (see any relevant checklist)? • reduce the risks as far as is reasonably practicable? If so, then the risks are adequately controlled; you should list below the precautions you have in place. You may refer to procedures or other documents in giving this information.	Describe any further risk reduction actions that you consider necessary. It may help to apply the principles below when discussing further action. If possible, try to: • remove the risk completely • try a safer option, e.g. use of aids, increased staffing • organize work to reduce exposure to hazard • consider what further training staff may need.	There is no hard and fast rule about when a review should be undertaken but a maximum of 12 months should be applied. It is important that once a review date has been agreed, it must be adhered to **but you do not have to wait until then to revise the arrangement if this proves necessary – it will depend on the actions you have decided upon.** You may need a different review date for each section listed in this assessment.

DATES FOR REVIEW	REVIEWED BY		NEW ACTIONS PLANNED	SEEN BY (enter initials)	DATE
	Name	Date			

(This part of the form is to be used when reviewing all or parts of the Risk Assessment)

If you are in domiciliary care and working in a person's home, then assessing and dealing with risks will be different for you.

If you feel that there is any kind of risk to the person you are supporting or to yourself, then you must tell your manager.

Hazardous Substances (Including Medication)

One important part of keeping the workplace safe is making sure that any hazardous substances are properly controlled. An important piece of health and safety legislation relates to the Control of Substances Hazardous to Health (COSHH).

COSHH states that the employer has a responsibility to identify how hazardous substances are handled, stored and disposed of safely. Hazardous substances include obvious things like bleach, but also items such as used syringes and medication. Locked cupboards are used to store items safely, and if you work in a residential setting and there should be a COSHH assessment form which names the items and how to store dispose of them safely (see a sample form on p.48).

> This piece of legislation will not apply if you are delivering care and support in a person's own home, but it is still important to control hazardous substances.

The symbols below can be found on bottles or containers containing hazardous substances and alert you to their danger.

Toxic   Harmful   Irritant   Corrosive

Below are some further symbols for hazards.

Explosive

Inflammable

Oxidizing

Hazardous substances must not be mixed, either when you are cleaning or using in a way that will mean the substances will come into contact with one another – for example in the pipes of the sink and toilet. This is because the substances might react with one another in a dangerous way.

SAFE DISPOSAL OF HAZARDOUS SUBSTANCES

Below is a list of substances that are hazardous with advice on how to dispose of them safely.

Hazardous substance	How to handle it	How to store it safely	How to dispose of it safely
Needles and syringes	Wear gloves	Keep locked in a medication cabinet	Use a 'sharps box'. Do not try to put the needle back into its sheath, instead put it straight into the sharps box. Do not empty this box. It should be replaced when nearly full and should never be allowed to overflow
Medication	Leave in its bottle or blister pack	Keep locked in medication cabinet	Return unused or out-of-date medication to chemist

Hazardous substance	How to handle it	How to store it safely	How to dispose of it safely
Bleach	Check with your manager first – some organizations do not like staff using bleach. Use gloves and an apron	Keep locked in cupboard	Rinse the bottle out. If there is any bleach that you wish to dispose of, dilute it and pour it down the sink or drain
Used dressings	Wear gloves and apron if needed	Should not be stored	Place in clearly labelled yellow bags
Body fluids (urine, faeces, blood, vomit)	Wear gloves and apron if needed	Should not be stored	Flush down the toilet. Put used gloves and apron in designated bin and wash your hands
Soiled linen	Wear gloves and apron if needed	Keep this in a bag. Use red bags as these can go straight into the washing machine (for more on bags and colour coding, see p.56)	
Paint			Paint left in a rolling tray or in a tin can be taken to your local recycling centre

> When using or storing any hazardous substance, remember to keep the original containers and labels

RISK ASSESSMENT OF HAZARDOUS SUBSTANCES

Each hazardous substance in the workplace needs to be risk assessed on a COSHH form (see example on p.48) because of the harm it could cause – for example, if a hazardous liquid were to get in someone's eyes or were accidentally ingested.

Sample COSHH assessment

Substance	Hazard(s)	Who is at risk and how	Can it be replaced with 'safe' substance?	Control Measures e.g. storage, protective clothing, training
Petrol for lawnmower	Risk of fire or explosion	Gardener, other individuals, because they often use the garage and could potentially have contact with the substance	No	1. Ensure no more than one gallon is stored in correctly marked container. 2. Keep container in locked cupboard (metal). 3. Issue written 'no smoking' instructions.

Date of assessment: . . . . Name: . . . .

Date for review:. . . . .

It is important that you know where the completed COSHH assessment forms are kept and that you are familiar with them in case you need to refer to them.

✎ Take some time now to look at your organization's policy on COSHH.

These forms should be reviewed every six months. Have yours been reviewed within this timescale?   Yes/No

Where is the locked cupboard?. . . . .

. . . .

Where is the key? . . . .

. . . .

Who has access to the key?. . . . .

. . . .

. . . .

✍ Take your organization's COSHH form to the locked cupboard where you keep hazardous substances. Is there any substance in the cupboard that is not on the COSHH form? Yes/No

If you have answered 'Yes', list below the substances and tell your manager or supervisor immediately.

. . . .

. . . .

. . . .

MEDICATION

Medication is hazardous if taken in the wrong measure, by the wrong person or in the wrong way. You are not allowed to administer medication until you have completed the necessary training. Once you have been trained to administer medication you must remember the six Rs:

Right person	Right time	Right medication
Right dose	Right record	Right method/route

Read your organization's policy on giving medication.

✍ Who is authorized to give medication to the people you support?

. . . .

. . . .

. . . .

✍ What can happen if a member of staff administers medication and he or she has not been trained to do so?

. . . .

. . . .

. . . .

Staff medication

The medication policy may say what you need to do if you are taking any kind of medication and where you should keep it safe while you are working. If you are on medication but you do not need to take any during the course of your work, you should still inform your manager in case:

- there are any side effects
- the medication can or might cause you to be drowsy.

Infection Control, Disease and Cleanliness

You will now read about infections and disease, how they commonly arise and how to minimize disease and infections; this will include advice on effective hand-washing and recommendations for cleaning.

FOOD

Within your role you will be supporting people with their personal care and may be cooking snacks and meals. There are risks associated with these – for example, the potential risk of infection from poor personal care, or of food poisoning if food is not cooked correctly. Disease may be present and, if it is, it can spread.

If food is not stored or cooked correctly, it can have bacteria on it or be contaminated with poison.

Food poisoning is brought about by the consumption of contaminated drink or food. The main symptoms will usually be diarrhoea, vomiting, stomach pains and nausea, in any combination.

The causes of food poisoning are bacteria, viruses and other poisons.

Bacteria

Living organisms can produce at alarming rates on food in the right circumstances. Bacteria are a major cause of food poisoning. Bacteria in large numbers are not visible to the naked eye. You could get 20,000 bacteria on the full stop at the end of this sentence.

Some types of bacteria protect themselves against conditions that would usually kill them by developing spores. Later, if the conditions are right, the spores turn into the bacteria and grow rapidly.

Bacteria are living things and need four things to survive and live:

- food
- warmth
- moisture
- time.

Viruses

Virus grow only on living tissue. You will not be able to see them with the naked eye. Although it is not entirely clear how virus activity affects food poisoning, what is clear is that many of the measures taken to prevent infectious diseases and fighting bacteria will lower the risk of a virus spreading.

Other poisons

Other poisons could include chemicals used to treat or grow food. Some fungi or plants are poisonous to humans. Certain seafood can have elements that can cause harm. For example, fresh crab or tuna need care when preparing to avoid certain parts that present a risk to health. Careful selection and washing are precautions that will reduce the risk of harm.

High-risk foods

Some foods are very high risk often because they are high in protein, contain moisture and, if not stored at the correct temperature, can cause bacterial growth. Some examples of high-risk foods are the following:

- Cooked meat, raw meat, gravy, stock and soups.
- Milk, eggs and products made from them.
- Shellfish, which is often eaten raw, as it may have come from contaminated water.
- Rice can produce spores that are resistant to cooking and if there is a delay after cooking the rice and before it is eaten or refrigerated, the bacteria can grow.

Moisture

Many foods contain moisture. Bacteria are unlikely to grow in dried food, but if bacteria do survive then adding moisture will begin the process again. When moisture is turned to ice it is no longer available to bacteria. However, as soon as the ice melts, the bacteria can use the moisture again.

Warmth

Bacteria that cause food poisoning will grow between 5° and 63° Celsius. Cooking over 70° Celcius will kill most bacteria, providing it is cooked through to the centre. The temperature has to be held for a length of time. Some bacteria and poisons require longer than others before they die.

Time

This is simply a matter of multiplication. One bacterium will split into two, then two into four, four into eight, eight into 16, 16 into 32 and so on. To grow, most bacteria need to be in the temperature range of 5° to 63° Celsius. The longer food is left in these conditions, the more they grow. Bacteria reproduce about every 15 minutes. They will stop growing when you control the conditions they need to grow.

Bacteria:

- like warmth

- are usually killed by heat

- can often survive cold to grow again.

Food poisoning can be caused in one of three ways:

- Bacteria that grow through the food we eat.

- Bacteria that are not killed by heat.

- Bacteria that have their own toxins, which are then released into our food before we eat it.

Common bacteria (and causes of food poisoning) include the following:

- *Salmonella*

- *Staphylococcus aureus*

- *Clostridium perfringens*

- *Campylobacter*

- *E. coli* (*Escherichia coli*)

- *Listeria.*

Sources of infection

Most bacteria come from human or animal sources; often the source is a carrier and does not display any signs. Humans can carry bacteria without knowing it.

If you use a knife to cut a piece of infected chicken and then cut the salad with the same knife, the chicken gets cooked but the salad does not, therefore the infection is on the salad.

> You cannot see, smell or notice bacteria.

Your manager will complete a RIDDOR form if there is a disease.

Precautions

To prevent disease and infection in relation to food please see pp.60–62.

PERSONAL CARE

Some staff see personal care as supporting individuals to use the toilet; however, it is more than this. Personal care is providing care and support, e.g. toileting, changing pads, supporting individuals who have cut themselves, etc. Coming into close contact with bodily fluids can increase the risk of cross-infection.

The risk of catching Hepatitis B may be increased when supporting some client groups. Your employer will advise that you have Hepatitis B and Tetanus injections, which should give you protection for a few years.

To reduce the risk of infection when offering personal care, ensuring high levels of personal hygiene is important; the next section will tell you how you can do this.

HOW TO CONTROL THE RISK OF INFECTION

Keeping a clean and hygienic working environment and good personal hygiene (both for yourself and the people you care for) will help to control the risk of infection. Make sure you follow your organization's health and safety policies and procedures, and also keep healthy and fit: this can help to keep immune levels up and reduce the risk of infection.

This section provides some practical advice on measures to take to control the risk of infection. First, it is worth thinking about how an infection commonly enters the body:

- inoculation by injection or being pricked by dirty needles

- being absorbed through the skin into the body and bloodstream

- open wounds and grazes

- insect bites

- ingestion, i.e. on food or eating

- inhalation, i.e. breathing

- sexual intercourse or bodily fluids.

The most obvious way of reducing the risk of infection is to reduce the likelihood of an infection being able to enter the body through any of the ways listed above. The following are simple measures that can be taken to reduce the risk:

- wearing protective clothing when appropriate (more on this on p.55)

- wearing clean clothes to work

- washing your hands regularly (more on this below)

- doing simple things like covering your mouth when you cough

- telling your employer if you have any of the following as this can be a sign of infection: an ear, nose or eye discharge, nausea, vomiting or diarrhoea.

USING PERSONAL PROTECTIVE EQUIPMENT

The Personal Protective Equipment at Work Regulation 1992 concerns the use of protective equipment. The main requirement of this regulation is that personal protective equipment must be supplied and worn at work wherever there are risks to health and safety that cannot be adequately controlled in other ways.

One way to prevent infection is to wear personal protective equipment (PPE). Examples of PPE include the following:

- disposable gloves (check the gloves before you wear them; they are no good to you if they have a hole in them)

- disposable aprons

- masks (if appropriate)

- rubber gloves.

The wearing of gloves can act as a barrier and whether you wish to wear them or not, it is advisable that this protective 'clothing' is worn for your own health and safety and that of the people you are supporting.

Please note that PPE is worn when doing a task. It does not mean that you should walk around the building wearing disposable gloves with your hands in the air and looking like a surgeon!

Wearing PPE when caring for people

The following is a list of tasks that all require PPE to be used:

- bathing

- changing soiled bed linen

- dealing with open sores and dressing wounds

- supporting a person to the toilet or commode

- putting cream on someone who has a skin condition, e.g. eczema, psoriasis

- dealing with incontinence or infections

- any other situations that expose you to a risk of infection.

Assisting an individual with bathing

- Make the person feel comfortable: ask the individual what level of support he or she wants, or check the care plan and consider if he or she wants to have a conversation or would prefer silence.

- Use disposable wipes on the lower body if the individual has been incontinent.

- Wash the individual starting from the head down to the feet and using different flannels or cloths. Wash from the face down to the upper body and after washing the upper body, change the water and use a clean flannel or cloth to wash the lower half of the body.

Dealing with soiled items

- Wearing gloves, bag the incontinence pad and put it in the designated bin.

- Cover soiled clothing or bedding and take to the laundry. Do not put the items on the floor. If it is your responsibility to wash the items, place items in the red bag and place the red bag in the washing machine. When the cycle begins the bag will split open and wash the items. When washing is complete place the used red bag inside another bag and dispose of it in the outside bin.

- The wash should be done on the highest temperature that the items can stand. It is important that you check the label in the item for instructions on how to wash them.

- Keep soiled items away from the kitchen.

- Bag any soiled items, using a yellow bag for clinical waste or a red bag for soiled linen.

HAND-WASHING

Washing your hands is the single most important task you can do to prevent infection.

You must wash your hands after carrying out any activity in which you are likely to be in contact with bacteria. This includes:

- at the start and end of your shift

- before and after wearing gloves

- after blowing your nose or sneezing

- after going to the toilet

- before and after eating

- when providing personal care.

Wash your hands between activities!

> Carry alcohol rub with you and use it when you cannot get to a sink to wash your hands. However, please note that the alcohol rub is not a substitute for washing your hands!

HOW TO WASH HANDS PROPERLY

- Wet hands under running water.

- Apply cleansing agent.

- Rinse well under running water.

- Dry thoroughly on disposable paper towels. If this is not practicable in your workplace, use a clean towel.

As paid staff, you do not have a choice of washing your hands or not. You must follow standards and wash your hands.

The people you support should be encouraged to wash their hands, but they can choose not to wash their hands or not to wash them as regularly as they should do to prevent infection. You cannot force the people you support to wash their hands but you can inform them that they have a responsibility like everyone else not to spread infection and they can do this by washing their hands regularly.

You can also provide the information, in their preferred method of communication, to enable the people you support to weigh up the pros and cons on washing or not washing hands. The people you support may wash their hands when they see you doing it. You can provide alcohol rub for the people you support.

If there is a great risk of infection by the people you support not washing their hands then you will need to discuss this with your manager, who will consider completing a risk assessment.

> Hot water and a pump soap should be available at all times.

1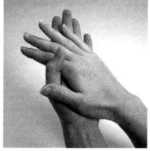

Palm to palm

2

Right palm over left dorsum and
left palm over right dorsum

3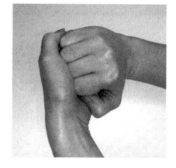

Palm to palm, fingers interlaced

4

Backs of fingers to opposing
palms with fingers interlaced

5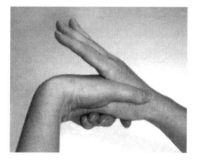

Rotational rubbing of right thumb
clasped in left palm
and vice versa

6

Rotational rubbing of right palm
with clasped fingers
and vice versa

Six steps in handwashing

CLEANLINESS

Remember, it is not just people who infect you. It can be anything, including objects in the workplace and particularly those which are breeding grounds for bacteria – for example a telephone, keyboard of a computer, a wheelchair, commode, hoist or even a tea caddy.

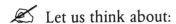 Let us think about:

- Getting a tea bag out of a container to make a cup of tea. If it is a narrow-headed container how many times did you accidentally touch other tea bags?

- There is a bowl of peanuts on a table. How many people have been to the toilet and did not wash their hands before taking some peanuts and leaving those that they accidentally touched with their unwashed hands?

- How many times do you use your mobile phone without washing your hands first? Do you wipe germs off it each time you get it out of your bag or pocket or when you have dropped it on the floor?

- How often are slings cleaned?

- How many times do you and others touch a person's hairbrush? How often is it cleaned?

As well as objects, spillages can provide opportunities for bacteria to grow and can also potentially be hazardous. Spillages should be dealt with quickly and your organization's policy will give you details on how to do this successfully, e.g. details of the chemicals to use.

Companion animals can be a person's best friend, but they can also present a risk of infection. They are good company and the lives of many people can be enriched through therapeutic partnerships with dogs, cats and other companion animals. The downside is that they can transfer micro-organisms when they come into a clean house after being out and getting dirty. It is important that animals are not allowed in the kitchen or anywhere near people's faces, that you wash your hands after coming into contract with an animal, and, if the animal has fleas or some other infestation, it is treated.

In large residential services there will be a cook and one or more staff who are responsible for cleaning. In smaller residential services cleaning the house will be part of your role to support the people who live there. There is probably a cleaning rota in your place of work and this can guide you on what needs to be washed and cleaned and its frequency. The cleaning rota may be divided into:

- daily and weekly washing

- daily, weekly, monthly, three-monthly and six-monthly cleaning.

The following is a guide on what needs to be washed or cleaned in the workplace, thinking about each room and special considerations for each.

CLEANING THE KITCHEN

- Wash your hands before serving food and after touching raw meat.

- Use different cleaning cloths for the kitchen, toilets and bathrooms. Some homes have orange cloths for the kitchen, blue cloths to clean the toilets and pink cloths to clean the bathroom sinks.

- Use different mops and buckets for the kitchen, bathroom and toilets. This can be achieved by putting a piece of tape with the word 'kitchen', etc.on them. You may think that you will buy another mop that is different to the one you already have, but how will agency staff know which one to use?

- Use a separate sink for hand-washing.

- Use a foot-operated bin so that you do not need to touch the bin to open it. All bins should have a plastic bag lining the inside. When the bag is full, it should be tied and put in the outdoor dustbin.

- Wear an apron, gloves and hairnet if required.

- Wear coloured plasters if you have any cuts or sores, as this will prevent you spreading bacteria into the food. Keep the cut or sore clean and wear a coloured plaster so that you will be able to see it if it comes off.

- Refrain from wearing:
  - nail varnish as you cannot see if there is dirt under your finger nails
  - false nails as dirt can accumulate underneath and/or they could fall off, or you could catch them on someone or something
  - false eye lashes or facial jewellery as these could come off
  - hand jewellery such as rings as dirt can get underneath (a wedding ring is an exception).

- Have a designated preparation area where you will prepare food. This area should be cleaned every time before it is used.

- Use different coloured chopping boards:
  - yellow for cooked meat
  - red for raw meat
  - blue for raw fish
  - white for dairy products and bakery
  - green for salad and fruit products
  - brown for vegetables.

- Clean the kettle regularly on the outside and descale it periodically. (The frequency will depend on the hardness of the water in your area.)

Washing up

- Crockery and other items should be allowed to air dry, but if this is not possible, use a clean tea towel and change it regularly.

- Ensure the dish drainer is cleaned regularly.

- Ensure the sharp ends of knives are not sticking up from the cutlery compartment of the dish drainer as people could catch their hands or arms on them and cut themselves.

- Even if you have a dishwasher where you work, the people you support may wish to learn how to do the washing up or perhaps they know how to do it and wish to maintain these skills. Your manager will have added this to the risk assessment for the kitchen.

- Change tea towels and cleaning cloths regularly. Single-use disposable cloths help to prevent the risk of infection.

Cooking

- Clean the cooker regularly.

- If you are using oven-cleaner to clean the oven, please ensure the area is ventilated and the people you support are not in the area while you are using it.

Fridge and freezer

- Label opened food with date of opening, use by date and what the product is.

- If opened food is in a tin, empty the contents of the tin into a container, cover it, label and place in the fridge.

- Put dairy items like cakes on the top shelf.

- Put raw meats in a covered dish on the bottom shelf to stop the juices dripping onto other foods.

- Check expiry dates on foods: food past its expiry date should be thrown away.

- Clean the fridge regularly.

- Monitor fridge and freezer temperatures at least once a day
  - fridge temperature should be between 1°C and 5°C
  - freezer temperatures should be -18°C.

Fridge and freezer temperatures should usually be checked either during the night by the night staff or by the early shift when they first come on duty and the temperature recorded. There can be times when the temperature has been taken and the reading is too high. This can be for many reasons, e.g. a faulty fridge or a broken door seal, or perhaps someone has opened the fridge door prior to you opening it to read the temperature. If the temperature is higher than it should be, record it along with the date and time it was checked and go back a little while later (making sure no one has opened the door in the mean time), take the temperature again and enter it again on the record sheet. If it continues to read high then you will need to discuss it with your manager. A useful tip to remember: to ascertain if a seal is broken, you can do a visual check or hold a bank note between the fridge or freezer door and its frame. If the bank note stays in place, then the seals are adequate.

Toaster

- The toaster needs to be emptied of crumbs regularly and checked for any bits of bread stuck inside it, otherwise this could cause a fire to start.

- Having bread stuck in the toaster could also cause a service user to put a knife in the toaster to remove it, presenting a risk of electrocution.

- Make sure the toaster is unplugged before attempting to clean it.

- Remove and empty the tray which catches most of the crumbs, then turn the toaster upside down and shake it.

Microwave oven

The microwave needs to be cleaned regularly. Don't forget to clean the inside roof of the microwave, as this gets dirty too!

CLEANING THE BATHROOM

- Toilet, bath and wash basin need to be cleaned regularly. The bath should be cleaned after each use.

- Floor should be mopped.

- Mats need to be washed regularly.

- Bin should be emptied and washed.

- Cabinet should be cleaned inside and out.

CLEANING THE LOUNGE

- Shelves, picture frames, ornaments, TV, etc. should be dusted.
- Carpet needs to be vacuumed.
- Bin should be emptied and washed.

CLEANING THE BEDROOM

- Combs, hairbrushes and razors need to be cleaned regularly.
- The toothbrush mug needs to be washed regularly.
- After supporting an individual to clean his teeth or gums (individuals with no teeth like to have fresh breath and massaging the gums goes some way to keeping them healthy), clean the brush in running water and place upright and leave to dry. Do not dry it on a towel.
- Sheets, quilt covers, pillowcases and towels need to be washed frequently.
- Quilts and pillows will also need to be cleaned occasionally, depending on their composition.
- Mattresses need to be vacuumed regularly and turned occasionally.
- Headboard can be vacuumed or sponged down (depending on which type it is).
- Bins need to be emptied and washed regularly.
- Mirrors, clocks, photo and picture frames, shelves and ornaments should be dusted.
- Carpet should be vacuumed.

CLEANING THE STAFF BEDROOM AND OFFICE

- Unplug the computer and clean the keyboard and mouse: you might think it does not need cleaning but try unplugging it and turning it over and shaking it to see what comes out of it! When cleaning a computer mouse, remove the ball and clean it.
- Telephone should be cleaned (key pad, telephone handset and mouth piece).
- Bedding should be washed after each night's sleep (unless you are sleeping in for two or more nights).
- Mattress should be vacuumed and turned periodically.
- Headboard can be vacuumed or sponged down (depending which type it is).

- Pillow should be washed periodically, depending on its composition.

- Carpet should be vacuumed.

- Dust any shelves, picture frames, ornaments, etc.

USING THE LAUNDRY ROOM

- Wash each service user's clothes separately.

- Regularly empty and clean the vacuum cleaner.

- Defluff tumble drier.

- Unplug the iron, clean it externally and descale periodically.

- Empty and clean bins regularly. The contents will affect how often the bins should be cleaned. Where possible put a clean bin bag inside the bin each time it is washed.

GENERAL POINTS

Don't forget to clean the lampshades, windows, doors and skirting boards occasionally!

As with hand-washing, you cannot force the people you support to keep areas free from infection but you can provide the information to enable them to weigh up the pros and cons. You will need to know how the individual prefers to communicate. You can provide literature if required showing the individual what can happen if the area is not kept clean. Sometimes people will follow what you do: if you clean up behind you, others may do the same.

It is important to note here that the home should be kept clean to reduce infection, but this does not mean that it needs to look like a show home. It is where the service users live and the home will look like it is lived in, and this is fine.

If the people you support do not follow your good practice and there is a great risk of infection, then you will need to discuss this with your manager, who will consider completing a risk assessment form.

How often are the areas below cleaned at your place of work?

Fridge

Door handle . . . .

Inside. . . . .

Seals . . . .

Fridge thermometer checked. . . . .

Freezer

Door handle . . . .

Inside. . . . .

Seals . . . .

Freezer thermometer checked . . . .

Frequency of being defrosted . . . .

Kitchen

Main door and its handles. . . . .

Cupboard insides. . . . .

Cupboard handles. . . . .

Cupboard doors . . . .

Sink and taps. . . . .

Floor . . . .

Vegetable rack . . . .

Cooker . . . .

Microwave oven . . . .

Dishwasher . . . .

Washing-up bowl . . . .

Dish drainer . . . .

Kitchen waste bin . . . .

Recycling bins . . . .

Lounge

Carpet vacuumed . . . .

Carpet steamed or deep cleaned . . . .

TV . . . .

Lampshades and light bulbs . . . .

Toilet

Toilet bowl . . . .

Wash basin . . . .

Basin taps . . . .

Floor . . . .

Waste bin . . . .

Bathroom

Bath. . . . .

Bath taps . . . .

Shower head . . . .

Shower curtain . . . .

Wash basin . . . .

Basin taps . . . .

Floor . . . .

Waste bin. . . . .

✍ Are there:

Separate mops and buckets to use for the toilets and kitchen?	Yes/No
Separate cloths for the kitchens, bathrooms and toilets?	Yes/No

If you have answered 'No' to these, what can you do about it? . . . .

. . . .

. . . .

Don't forget... if there are cobwebs they need to be removed.

Safe Manual Handling

The Manual Handling Operations Regulations 1992 (amended 2002) require that if there is a risk of injury with manual handling, then it should be reduced as far as possible. Policies and procedures should be put in place to prevent back injuries caused by improper manual handling.

Under these regulations employers must carry out a risk assessment for manual handling and the equipment that is to be used. The assessment will be written on a risk assessment form and will include information on how to reduce the risks and how staff should use the equipment provided. It will have a date on it when it should be reviewed.

Your employer is also required to provide specific training if your job involves moving the people you support. Every job will require you to do some form of moving and handling.

MOVING PEOPLE

If you are required to move a person, it is always a good idea to try to consider the service user and think about how it would feel from his point of view.

If using a sling, it is very important that you are aware how daunting and frightening it may be for some individuals to be manoeuvred by a piece of equipment or a hoist which looks like a crane.

During your training, ask if you can sit in the sling and be moved from one spot to the next.

Good practice if you have to move an individual

- Ensure you have completed your training.

- Inform the individual what you are going to do.

- Explain in a way the individual can understand.

- Ask the individual for permission to carry out the move.

- If the move requires two people, ensure there are two of you present to carry out the move.

- Remember to bend your knees, not your back – *do not* twist your body as this could damage your spine.

- Use the equipment provided.

You must not do any moving of people or use any equipment until you have received training. When you receive training you will learn how to use the range of equipment appropriate to your work: slings, hoists, swivel aids, transfer boards, slide sheets, leg-lifters, trapeze handles, and so on.

It is important that the service user has a say in how he or she wishes to be moved and the individual's care plan will inform you which equipment is to be used for each individual.

If the service user wants you to move him or her without the equipment, you must inform your manager. You could injure yourself and/or the service user if you do not use the equipment provided. You will need to ask the service user why he or she wants to be moved without the equipment. There will be a reason (maybe the person does not feel safe, it has hurt him or her in the past, etc).

MOVING OBJECTS

It is inevitable that you will move objects around the workplace. Whether heavy or not, you should still think about the health and safety risks involved in moving objects and reduce them where you can. Examples can be anything that needs to be picked up or moved, whether a box, a shopping bag, some potatoes, etc.

Good practice if you have to move an object

- Assess the object: can you grip it? Can it be lifted?

- Assess the environment: where does the object need to be moved to? Is the floor even? Is the space wide enough? Is the floor slippery?

- Remember to bend your knees, not your back – *do not* twist your body as this could damage your spine.

- Keep feet wide apart so you are stable.

- Hold load close to body.

- Use equipment provided.

- If you are carrying shopping, divide the shopping between two bags and carry one bag in each hand.

Your manager will ask you to complete training on 'inanimate loads' and a way of remembering the four aspects of handling objects that your training will cover is the four **P**s:

Picking up   Putting down   Pushing   Pulling

CHECKING EQUIPMENT

You must check the equipment every time you go to use it. You must be vigilant and if you have any concerns while using the equipment you must stop immediately, ensure the service user is safe and report your concerns.

The Lifting Operations and Lifting Equipment Regulations 1998 (LOLER) are the regulations that cover equipment. Under these regulations employers have a responsibility to ensure that equipment is:

- used safely

- the right type of equipment for the right purpose

- installed safely

- checked regularly by a competent person:

    ° annual checking for inanimate objects

    ° six-monthly checks on equipment used more regularly in moving and handling people.

The competent person will then submit a report following a thorough inspection.

RISK ASSESSMENT FOR MANUAL HANDLING

A risk assessment should be in place for all moving and positioning of people or objects. The risk assessment will show:

- the risk to the person being lifted

- the risk to the person(s) carrying out the move

- the measures put in place to reduce the risk

- resources and equipment needed and in place

- the review date.

The process of assessing a risk involves the following actions:

- looking for potential hazards

- deciding who might be harmed

- deciding how the person might be harmed

- determining what is the likelihood of the risk

- deciding on ways to reduce or remove the risk

- deciding who else needs to be informed

- recording all of the above on the appropriate risk assessment form

- reviewing regularly.

If your workplace does not require you to do this, you may think that you do not need any training: *this is not the case.*

✍ Stop for a minute and answer this: you have just dropped a pen on the floor and you pick it up. How do you do this safely?

. . . .

. . . .

. . . .

. . . .

Looking after Yourself

It is important to take care of yourself as well as others when in the workplace. This applies to your body and your mind.

LOOKING AFTER YOUR BACK

It is very important that you look after your spine. Following the advice given on manual handling about the correct way to lift objects or move people will go a long way in helping you to look after your spine.

You can injure yourself if you:

- stretch to reach something

- carry items for a long period, e.g. shopping bags

- twist your body

- bend over from the waist rather than bending your knees.

If you require more information you can:

- look at your organization's policies and procedures

- ask your manager or colleagues

- ask your health and safety representative for advice

- contact the union health and safety representative if you belong to a union

- log on to the Internet and visit the government's Health and Safety Executive website at www.hse.gov.uk

---

You only have one spine – look after it!

SMOKING AND DRINKING

While it is your choice to decide whether or not to smoke or drink outside of work, organizations will have guidance on both activities in the workplace. All organizations will have a no-smoking policy for its staff to follow.

Drinking policy can vary from one organization to another. Some have a no-drinking policy for before or during work. Other organizations allow some alcohol when you are out with a service user: the policy will state how much can be consumed.

STRESS

There is some stress in every job regardless of what level of position you hold. There are two types of stress:

- 'rusted out' refers to when the skills of the employee are not being used

- 'burnt out' refers to when an employee is stressed due to working very long hours or in a particularly stressful, high-pressure job.

You need to inform your manager or supervisor if you or the people you support have any problems and/or stress related to work.

It is important that you do this because your manager or supervisor needs to know how you and the people you support are feeling. By telling him or her the problems, you can discuss together what can be done to reduce the stress levels.

It is said that a little stress is good for the body but too much stress could have an effect on the service you provide to the people you support, your colleagues and cause ill health to yourself.

> In 2007/08 an estimated 442,000 individuals in Britain, who worked in the last year, believed that they were experiencing work-related stress at a level that was making them ill, according to the Labour Force Survey (LFS). (Health and Safety Executive 2008)

The Working Time Regulations policy

Stress can be caused by staff working too many hours. The Working Time Regulations policy states the number of hours employees should work and their annual leave entitlement. Your organization will have a policy on this and you can obtain more information by going onto the Department for Business Enterprise and Regulatory Reform (BERR) website at www.berr.gov.uk/whatwedo/ employment/employment-legislation/working-time-regs (accessed on 17 December 2008).

✍ Here are some symptoms of stress. You may like to circle the ones that apply to you and show this page to your manager or supervisor.

Crying for no reason   Feeling pessimistic and unhappy

Increased anxiety

Taking days off work

Headaches

Feeling indecisive

Being irritable

Loss of sexual appetite   Spread easily

Feeling tense and strained

Muscle tension

Lack of concentration

Stomach cramps or upset stomach

Waking between 2 a.m. and 4 a.m.

Lack of self-worth

Increased use of stimulants e.g. tea/coffee/cigarettes/food

Discuss the ringed problems with your supervisor and devise strategies to help you deal with stress for yourself, the people you support and the staff you work with.

. . . .

. . . .

. . . .

. . . .

. . . .

You will feel better within yourself if you can get plenty of fresh air and exercise and follow a good diet.

HARASSMENT AND BULLYING

Under the Health and Safety Act 1974 it is illegal for a staff member to harass or bully another staff member. Your employer should have a policy in place to inform everyone that it is unacceptable to harass or bully others and that this can lead to disciplinary action.

The policy should also tell you who to go to if this is happening to you, such as your manager, and also details of who to contact if it is your manager who is bullying or harassing you, such as Human Resources or the deputy manager.

WORKING WITH COMPUTERS

Your manager will have a policy in place for you to read which will give guidance on how to sit at the computer, the position of the computer and so on.

 Please have a look at this policy now.

Risk assessment

Your manager will complete a risk assessment form with you if you are a computer user. These forms can vary from one organization to another but generally they will cover these areas:

- space
- lighting
- chair
- desk

- foot rest

- display screen

- keyboard.

Incorrect use can cause:

- headaches

- tiredness

- dry and itchy eyes

- back ache.

Eye care

If you use a computer a lot during your working day you may be entitled in law to receive an eyesight test at the expense of your organization.

VEHICLE SAFETY

Many residential settings will have a company vehicle and many service users may have their own mobility car. These vehicles will require regular checks, e.g. water, oil, brake fluid and tyres. These 'vehicle checks' are usually carried out by a competent person in the workplace.

✍ Find out who is responsible for the check of the company vehicle and how often it is done. You may wish to ask the person if you can observe the next check.

. . . .

. . . .

✍ Driving the company vehicle may involve thinking about the following questions:

- Does the worker have a clean, current driving licence?

- Does the person need to pass a test for this vehicle (for instance if it is a minivan or ambulance).?

- Is the seat at the correct height and position for the driver?

- Can the driver reach the pedals, see the mirrors and have an unimpeded view?

. . . .

. . . .

. . . .

. . . .

If you are new to driving the company vehicle, you may wish to go for a short drive yourself to get used to the vehicle before taking individuals out in it.

Most vehicles have a book where you record your mileage (start and finish) and the reason for taking the people out that you support.

✍ If you are a driver, please discuss with your supervisor what checks you will need to do before taking the vehicle out.

. . . .

. . . .

. . . .

. . . .

Safety while driving

- Switch off your mobile phone while you are driving.

- Ensure that everyone wears a seatbelt. If anyone refuses, inform your manager immediately and do not take the vehicle out.

✍ Is there a risk assessment in place for the vehicle?   Yes/No

Discuss the vehicle risk assessment with your supervisor.
Does it cover behaviour of passengers likely to distract the driver,
breakdowns, accidents etc?   Yes/No

Does the vehicle have a plan in it to tell you what to do in the case
of an accident?   Yes/No

Have you read it?   Yes/No

. . . .

. . . .

. . . .

. . . .

Emergencies in the Workplace

This section covers what you will need to do in the event of an emergency. There are many types of emergencies, and how you deal with them will differ depending on where you are working.

EMERGENCY PLAN OR DISASTER PLAN

In residential settings there will be plans on what to do if there is an emergency; some call them 'disaster plans'.

For example, a fire or gas leak may mean you cannot get back into the building for some time or (depending on the damage) not for a very long time. If this happens you need to know where to take the people you support. If you have this plan in place, you should be familiar with it and know if your manager has agreed with a local hotel, caravan site, sports hall or similar place that in the event of an evacuation, the people you support can stay there for the night.

The plan will be in an envelope or folder near the front and back doors and will have the following information in it:

- names and dates of birth of all service users

- names and telephone numbers of all staff (so they can be called in an emergency)

- details of local doctor and medication

- names and telephone numbers of service users' relatives

- names and telephone numbers of others, e.g. social worker, community nurse, advocate, plumber, electrician, gas engineer and so on

- service users' food allergies

- spare set of car keys (for the company vehicle).

ELECTRICAL EMERGENCIES

If a person is electrocuted:

- Do not panic.

- Turn off and unplug the appliance.

- *Do not* touch the person until the electricity is disconnected.

- If you cannot turn off the electricity, stand on a mat or dry newspapers and use a wooden or plastic broom handle to move the casualty away from the current.

- Call for the first-aider on shift or dial 999.

- The trained first-aider will give mouth-to-mouth resuscitation if the casualty is not breathing.

- Keep the person warm.

- Inform your manager and the service user's next of kin.

- Complete an accident form.

If an electrical appliance catches fire:

- Unplug the appliance or turn off power at the mains.

- Follow the fire procedure.

- Inform your manager.

- Complete an incident form.

When the electricity goes off for no known reason:

- Check the mains box.

- Identify why it went off. Sometimes it may not be apparent; in this case, check the last item used, e.g. the toaster.

- Inform your manager.

- Complete an incident form.

✍ Ask your supervisor to show you where the switches for the fuse box are and where you can access the emergency electrician telephone number.

. . . .

. . . .

. . . .

General tips on electricity

- When buying new items with plugs or light bulbs ensure that fuses or bulb wattage are correct.

- Handle electrical equipment only with dry hands.

- *Fully* unreel extension leads before use.
- Check electrical tools and their flexible leads or cords before use.

The Electricity at Work Regulations 1989

All electrical equipment should be maintained by a competent person. Your employer should arrange for all fixed electrical equipment to be inspected every five years.

General maintenance

In your private life, you may change a light bulb, rewire a plug, decorate and wallpaper the hall, etc. Although you might do this in your own house, please be aware that you cannot do this where you work unless it is within your role and you have undergone training. You may wish to discuss this further with your manager.

✎ What does your policy say you should do if equipment is faulty?

. . . .

. . . .

. . . .

. . . .

✎ What should you do with the equipment while waiting for it to be repaired?

. . . .

. . . .

. . . .

. . . .

FIRE EMERGENCIES

✎ Locate your policy and procedure on what to do if there is a fire. It may say something like this:

1. Sound the alarm.

2. Evacuate everyone from the building to the assembly point (in accordance with agreed procedure).

3. There may be a risk assessment in place where some non-ambulant clients will stay in the building behind fire doors.

4. Ensure the Fire Brigade is called.

5. Once the alarms are ringing, *do not silence them* – the brigade will do this when they arrive.

6. Senior staff member should inform the Fire Brigade if anyone is left in the building.

7. Do not re-enter the building until told to do so.

8. Count heads and report to senior staff member on duty.

9. Inform your manager.

10. Complete a health and safety incident form.

How to reduce the risk of fire

Do not:

- permit service users to smoke in bed (inform your manager if this continues)
- leave lighted candles unattended
- leave pans cooking on the cooker
- overload electrical sockets
- leave plugs in electrical sockets
- leave cigarettes burning.

How to prevent a fire from spreading

- Close doors (fire doors should be kept closed at all times unless they are on magnets and will close automatically once the alarm goes off).
- Use a fire extinguisher if it is a small fire.
- Use a fire blanket on burning fat in a chip pan.

> Please note you should not use fire equipment if you have not been trained in how to use it.

Some residential homes have a direct line to the local fire station. How is the Fire Brigade called to your place of work?

. . . .

. . . .

. . . .

Who do you call if there is a fault with your fire alarm system?

. . . .

. . . .

. . . .

Fire fighting and using fire extinguishers

There are three ways to extinguish a fire:

- *Starvation*: if the fire is starved of fuel and it has nothing left to burn, it will die.

- *Smothering*: if the supply of oxygen is cut off or controlled, the fire will die.

- *Cooling*: if heat can be taken out of the fire, it will die.

Generally the fire extinguishers either smother or cool fires. You should attempt to fight only those fires that you are capable of fighting.

There are several types of fire extinguisher and it is important to ensure that you have the correct one for the fire that you are fighting. It can be very dangerous to use the wrong extinguisher, as explained below.

- Always test the extinguisher before approaching the fire in case it does not work.

- Always fight the fire with your back to your escape route.

- Ensure your escape route is clear.

- Avoid pushing or spreading the fire with the blast from the extinguisher.

- If you do not manage to extinguish the fire with the first extinguisher, consider it to be beyond your means and get out, closing all the doors behind you as you go.

- If in doubt, get out and stay out.

- Always call the Fire Brigade even if you have managed to put the fire out. They are the experts and will make sure the fire is properly extinguished.

A useful way of learning how to use a fire extinguisher is to remember **PASS**:

P   **P**ull the pin

A   **A**im low

S   **S**queeze the handle

S   **S**weep from side to side.

There are four main types of fire extinguisher: water, carbon dioxide, dry powder and foam.

Water extinguishers

- *Colour*: all red.

- *Extinguishing action*: cooling.

- *Designed to extinguish*: wood, paper, textiles.

- *Danger*: do not use on fuel, electrical, or chip pan fires, as this causes a violent reaction and will spread the fire dramatically.

Water extinguishers

- *Method of use*: the jet should be directed at the base of the flames and kept moving across the area of the fire. Any hot spots should be sought out after the main fire is extinguished.

Carbon dioxide extinguishers

- *Colour*: red with a black indicator band.

- *Extinguishing action*: smothering.

- *Designed to extinguish*: electrical fires and flammable liquids; safe and clean to use on live electrical equipment.

Carbon dioxide extinguishers

- *Danger*: has a limited cooling effect: take care to ensure the fire does not reignite. The gas used may be harmful: ventilate and evacuate the area as soon as the fire is extinguished.

- *Method of use*: the discharge horn should be directed at the base of the flames and kept moving across the area of the fire. Do not hold the horn, pipe or base of the extinguisher as they become very cold during operation.

Dry powder extinguishers

- *Colour*: red with blue indicator band.

- *Extinguishing action*: smothering and cooling.

- *Designed to extinguish*: electrical fires, flammable liquids, wood, paper, textiles; very effective on car-engine fires.

- *Danger*: do not use on chip pan fires; difficult to use in windy conditions; can cause extensive damage to electrical appliances; creates a lot of mess if used indoors; has a limited cooling effect and care must be taken to ensure the fire does not reignite.

Dry powder extinguishers

- *Method of use*: the discharge nozzle should be directed at the base of the flames and with a rapid sweeping motion the flames should be driven towards the far edge until they are out. If the extinguisher has a shut-off control, the air should be allowed to clear. If the flames reappear attack the fire again.

Foam

- *Colour*: red with a cream indicator band.

- *Extinguishing action*: smothering and cooling.

- *Designed to extinguish*: A class (solid materials such as wood and paper, and most textiles) and B class (all liquids or liquefied solids – fuels and oils) fires.

- *Danger*: do not use on live electrical equipment or chip pan fires; may be susceptible to burn back if not applied correctly. Avoid contact with the eyes because it is an irritant.

- *Method of use*: the jet should be directed on to a back edge or nearby surface above the burning liquid so that the foam can build up and flow across the liquid.

Foam extinguishers

General points

✍ How many smoke detectors, alarm points, extinguishers and fire exits are in the home? Please complete the following chart, stating where each one is located.

Smoke detectors	Alarm points	Extinguishers and what they are used for	Fire exits

✍ Ask your manager how often:

- the fire alarms should be tested and by whom

- the fire extinguishers, smoke detectors and electrical lighting should be tested and by whom

- fire drills should be carried out and who is responsible for carrying them out.

. . . .

. . . .

. . . .

. . . .

All this information is a requirement of the Commission for Social Care Inspection and needs to be recorded.

Please ask your manager where the records are kept and have a look at them.

Frequent fire drills will enable the people you support and you and your colleagues to know what to do in the event of an emergency. It will also give everyone the skills and knowledge to react calmly in an emergency situation.

It is important that the people you support understand the risk of fire and how to prevent a fire. This can be done by sitting down with the individual and discussing it either verbally or by using pictures or by watching a video or DVD on fire prevention.

Supporting people in their own home

People living in their own home will not have any organized fire drills. Along with discussing how to prevent a fire with the individual, you should also discuss with the individual how he or she would get out of the accommodation if there was a fire.

GAS EMERGENCIES

- If you smell gas, do not switch on a light because this could cause an explosion.

- Open doors and windows to let the fumes escape.

- Evacuate the building following the evacuation fire procedure, taking the disaster plan with you.

- Take a telephone out of the building and ring the emergency number.

 Ask your supervisor or manager:

- Where the emergency gas board number is.

- Where the key is kept to shut off the gas.

- Where the gas shut-off point is.

- What you need to do after an incident like this, i.e. recording and reporting.

- What to do if you are delivering care in an individual's home.

. . . .

. . . .

. . . .

. . . .

CORGI (Since 1 April 2009, Gas Safe Register has replaced CORGI gas registration as the official gas safety body) registered gas fitters must also report dangerous gas fittings they find, and gas conveyors/suppliers must report some flammable gas incidents. (Health and Safety Executive, at www.hse.gov.uk/riddor guidance.htm)

WATER EMERGENCIES AND FLOOD

- If there is a water leak, turn off the stopcock.

- Do not turn on a light or anything that is electrical.

- Turn off the electricity.

- Evacuate the building following the fire evacuation procedure, taking the disaster plan with you.

- Take a telephone out of the building and ring the emergency number for the plumber.

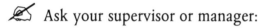 Ask your supervisor or manager:

- What you should do if there is a water leak or flood.

- Where the emergency number for the plumber is.

- Where the stopcock is to turn off the water.

- What you need to do after an incident like this, i.e. recording and reporting.

- What to do if you are delivering care in an individual's home.

· ·

· ·

· ·

· ·

· ·

> The telephone numbers for the electrician, gas and water board will be on the notice board or in your work's telephone contacts book and on the disaster plan.

HEALTH EMERGENCIES

We have already covered a number of hazards that could lead to health emergencies in the workplace. Here are some common problems:

- Slipping on a wet floor or on wet leaves in the garden.

- Burning yourself on steam from a kettle or the hob on the cooker.

- Using equipment incorrectly and hurting your back or the person you are moving.

- A staff member or service user having a health emergency, such as an epileptic seizure, heart attack or stroke.

- Someone having food poisoning.

- Someone being injured in a road accident.

First-aiders must be trained and should only give treatment in what they have been trained to do. There should be a notice saying where the first aid box is and who are the trained persons to administer first aid.

✎ It is important that you discuss *now* with your supervisor or manager the limits of your responsibility and what you can do and must not do when an emergency occurs.

. . . .

. . . .

. . . .

. . . .

General guidance

1. Remain calm.
2. Assess the situation. Make sure there is no danger to yourself or others.
3. Call for appropriate help. Do you need an ambulance, a GP, or advice from the senior member of staff on shift or the manager?
4. Give first aid if you have been trained to do so.
5. Make the area safe, i.e. nothing close to the individual so he cannot hurt himself further.
6. Do not move the individual unless advised to by a competent trained person.
7. Make the area private if you can, i.e. ask onlookers to go away.
8. Reassure the individual.
9. Give information to the paramedics when they arrive, e.g. what happened, medical history, current medication etc.

✍ Questions to think about:

Where is the first aid box kept? . . . .

Is it within easy reach of everyone?   Yes/No

Is there a first aid kit in the company vehicle?   Yes/No

Who is responsible for ensuring the first aid kit is complete?

. . . .

What are the expiry dates of the bandages and dressings? . . . .

. . . .

Have you received training in first aid yet?   Yes/No

If you have answered 'No', what is the date you are attending this training?

. . . .

Are you aware that you will need to do a refresher course
every three years?   Yes/No

✐ In your supervision, please discuss with your supervisor what you should do in the event of a death.

. . . .

. . . .

. . . .

. . . .

> It is important that you wear personal protective equipment when treating people who have had an accident which involves loss of blood and/or fluids, e.g. disposable gloves and resuscitation aids to prevent cross-infection.

BASIC FIRST AID TECHNIQUES

This section gives basic information on some first aid techniques. It is not a substitute for first aid training and your manager will inform you when you are booked on to a first aid course.

Checking for signs of breathing

1. Check for signs of breathing by looking for the chest to rise and fall.
2. Listen for breathing and feel for breath against your cheek.

The following steps should only be followed if there is no sign of breathing. If there is breathing, the casualty should be put in the recovery position.

Checking for breathing

Opening the airway

1. Tilt the head back.
2. Check for obstructions.
3. Lift the chin with two fingers.

Opening the airway

Giving rescue breaths

1. Open the casualty's airway.
2. Pinch casualty's nose so that it is firmly closed.
3. Take a deep breath and seal lips around the casualty's mouth.
4. Blow into the mouth until chest rises.
5. Remove mouth and allow the chest to fall.
6. Repeat once more then check for breathing again.
7. Check for breathing after every ten breaths.

Giving mouth to mouth

If breathing resumes, put the casualty in the recovery position.

Using the recovery position

1. Putting someone in the recovery position will prevent him from choking on vomit and keep his airway clear.
2. You would put someone in this position if he was unconscious but breathing. However, if there is a possibility that the person had a back or neck injury then you would not move him.

Recovery position

3. Kneel beside the casualty and remove sharp objects like keys from his clothing. With the casualty on his back open the casualty's airway by tilting his head and lifting his chin, straighten his legs, bend his near arm so that his arm is at right angles, bend his far leg keeping his foot on floor so the knee is bent upwards.
4. Place casualty's far arm across his chest, with the back of his hand against his cheek, gently pull the casualty's far knee and hip, rolling him towards you until he is lying on his side, tilt casualty's head to ensure airway is open.
5. Adjust upper leg so that hip and knee are at right angles to support the casualty, check airway and breathing.

Responding to bleeding

The aim is to control the bleeding, reduce the likelihood of infection and get medical attention as soon as possible.

1. Apply firm pressure, using a sterile dressing if possible.

2. Where possible e.g. with an arm or wrist injury, raise wound above heart level.

3. Apply sterile dressing and bandage firmly.

Responding to choking

The aim is to remove obstructions from the casualty's mouth as quickly as you can.

Back slap

1. Remove any dentures.

2. Sweep the casualty's mouth with one finger (gloved if possible) to clear any food from the mouth.

3. Encourage the casualty to cough.

4. If no result, stand behind the casualty and give five sharp slaps to the back between the shoulder blades.

5. If no result, stand behind the casualty and apply five abdominal thrusts: place arms around abdomen, bend forward slightly, put fist below base of breastbone, put other hand on top and pull sharply in and up five times. Listen for the obstruction being dislodged, check the mouth and remove matter.

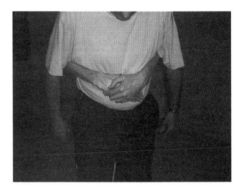

Abdominal thrust

Dealing with burns and scalds

1. If it is a major burn or scald, call for help immediately.

2. Place under slowly running cold water or immerse in water for a minimum of ten minutes (or 20 minutes if it is a chemical burn) as this will help to alleviate the pain and decrease the spread of heat.

3. If you can, remove any rings, clothes or shoes that are restrictive before the burned area begins to swell. Gently remove any clothing that is not burnt or stuck to the burn or scald.

4. If clothing is on fire: *stop, drop, wrap* and *roll* the person on the ground.

5. *Do not* remove any burnt clothing as this will now be sterilized due to it being burnt.

6. Cover the injured part, unless it is a burn or scald of the face, with a sterile dressing or a dry, clean non-adhesive dressing. If you do not have either of these, leave the burn or scald uncovered, unless it is on the person's foot or hand and it can be covered with a clean plastic bag or cling film.

Do not:

- prick blisters

- apply ointments, lotions, margarine or butter

- breathe over the burned areas

- touch the burned areas.

SUPPORT AFTER AN EMERGENCY

An emergency of any kind can be very distressing and you need to make sure that you support the individuals and your colleagues afterwards and that you get support for yourself.

There are a number of reasons why someone would be distressed, for example:

- The person is traumatized by what has happened.

- The individual witnessed the accident, saw the blood loss, saw the person on the stretcher and so on.

- The witness felt useless and unable to do anything.

- It was a relative or friend involved.

The person who is distressed will need support and this can vary depending on the individual, for example:

- One person may need to talk about it and want to talk about it continuously over the next few days or weeks.

- Another person may go to his or her bedroom and not wish to talk about it.

You will be asked by other people how the casualty is and you will need to reassure the people you support that he or she is being cared for. It is important that you do not give opinions or tell individuals something you are not trained to do, thus do not say 'He/she will be fine'.

You may need support yourself, and your manager will provide this for you, unless you prefer for it to be from someone else, perhaps a senior or your supervisor. When an incident or accident has occurred, it is quite common to reflect on what happened and wonder whether you could have done anything differently or better.

Taking time to review your own work is beneficial and discussing it in supervision is all part of good reflective practice. Supervision provides a safe environment in that these sessions are confidential and usually things discussed in the supervision meeting stay in the meeting.

Some information may need to passed on if, for example, you require professional counselling, or if there is an investigation. You will receive feedback in a supportive way from your supervisor in your supervision meetings.

Safety and Security

SAFETY AND SECURITY IN THE WORKPLACE

If you work in a residential setting, there will be a property sheet or book that will have a record of every individual's valuables and possessions. There will be a separate record for the individual's finances.

All visitors to a residential setting will be required to sign a visitors' book and give details of their name, who they have come to see and what time they arrived. They will sign out as they are about to leave and enter the time of leaving the building. This is to ensure that you know who is in the building and why, and it will be of great use if there is a fire.

You need to check that all visitors have a right to enter the premises. You can do this by checking their identification; if they do not have any with them, do not let them into the building until you have checked who they are.

The service user may not wish to see the relative or friend who has arrived at the front door and, where possible, the service user should tell the person why he or she does not wish to have visitors. It may be that they have had an argument, or just that it is not a convenient time to visit.

People who live in their own home may need prompting or reminding to ask for identification. The password schemes offered by some gas, electric and water companies are good because callers have to give a password before the individual will open the door.

In both private homes and residential homes, it is important that all outer doors have good locks on them and the main doors can be locked from the inside. Fire doors need to be opened from the inside in the event of a fire.

Doors can have spy holes which enable the person inside to see who is at the door before opening it. A chain on the door is another security feature; but should only be used when opening the door to an unknown person as it can be a clear danger if fastened when a fire, gas leak etc. occurs as not only can it delay exit, it can delay emergency services entering.

Windows must also have good locks on them and need to be secure. If they are wooden framed, the wood needs to be in good repair, if not, the wood could be weakened and chipped away and an intruder can get in. Security lighting and burglar alarms can also deter people who might want to enter.

Some service users or staff may like to have their downstairs windows open to let fresh air in. This could be a risk as an intruder can get in. To reduce this risk, you can discuss with the people you support about getting window locks which will enable the window to be opened just a few inches and no more.

If the people you support refuse to have these locks, you can discuss the risks with them. If solutions are not found you will need to discuss this with your manager, who will consider completing a risk assessment.

Many homes have a rota board on display to show which staff are on duty. Is this placed where visitors can see it? If it is you should think about moving it somewhere where visitors cannot see it. Visitors such as builders do not need to know how many staff are in the building, especially if staff are working the shift on their own.

✍ Have you been issued with a key to the workplace?   Yes/No

What happens to this key when you are off duty?

. . . .

. . . .

Have you been informed what to do if you are all going out one
evening (not necessarily together) and the home will be empty,
e.g. draw the curtains, keep a light on?   Yes/No

Does the front door have a code to get in?   Yes/No

If it does, how often is it changed?. . . . .

Is it changed each time a staff member leaves?   Yes/No

✍ Please ask your manager what you should do if there is an intruder in the building or trying to get into the building. Write your answer here:

. . . .

. . . .

. . . .

. . . .

LONE WORKING

✍ If you are a lone worker, have you read the risk assessment

on lone working?   Yes/No

If you answered 'No', please arrange a time to read it as soon as you can.

Have you been told that you must ensure the office or your
manager knows exactly where you at any time while you are working?   Yes/No

This is for your own safety. If you deviate from these times, you
must let the office or your manager know immediately.

Have you been issued with a mobile phone and/or panic alarm?   Yes/No

Have you been issued with an identification card?   Yes/No

Do you need any training on how to combat violence and aggression? Yes/No

SAFETY AND SECURITY OUTSIDE OF THE WORKPLACE

There are occasions when your safety may be threatened when you are outdoors.

Risky activity	What you can do to reduce this risk
Walking to your car after work in the dark	Park your car near to a well-lit area and have your key ready. If you have central locking, do not press the button on your key to unlock the doors before you get there as someone could jump in before you do.
Walking in the dark to the bus stop	Walk in well-lit areas, have a personal alarm with you, preferably in your coat pocket, have your bag zipped up and turned so the zips are nearest to your body or facing you.
Taking money to, or withdrawing money from, a bank	Do not put the money in a money bag, use a different bag or money belt. Tell colleagues where you are going and when you will be back. Keep the money in the bag until you go into the bank and reach the cashier. Carry a personal alarm and mobile phone. When withdrawing cash, put the money into your bag before leaving the cashier. Consider going to the bank in pairs.
Wearing headphones while walking in the street	Music can distract you from what is happening around you, and someone might want to steal a portable music player.
Carrying your laptop	If you carry your laptop in the specially designed laptop shoulder bag, everyone will know you have a laptop with you. Try using a different bag.
Using the train alone	Sit where others are sitting; try not to be in a carriage by yourself. If you are not sure where you are going, try not to show this when you are alone as you may indicate your vulnerability. If you have to consult a map, try to do so when others are not watching.

Risky activity	What you can do to reduce this risk
Using your mobile phone	Using a mobile phone can have its advantages and disadvantages. Using it can deter someone from approaching you as the potential attacker may think that you will let the person on the telephone know what is happening. Disadvantages are that it can distract you from what is happening around you. When using the phone the key pad lights up thus drawing attention to you, and if you are seen using an up-to-date phone it could be grabbed from you.

Letting people know where you are

It is important to let people know that you are leaving the building, where you are going, and the time you are likely to return. The reason for this is that, if you do not return when you say you will, your manager or colleagues will start wondering where you are and will start looking for you.

There may be times when one of the people you support leaves the building and does not return by the expected time. Reasons for this can vary, for example, the bus was late, they lost their way, they left the building and had no sense of direction. These cases naturally give cause for concern.

Your organization may have a missing person's policy and if it has you should read it. If you have not got one, please discuss with your manager what you should do if a service user or colleague leaves the building and does not return by the expected time. Write your answer here.

CHALLENGING BEHAVIOUR

You may be supporting individuals who present challenging behaviour, either in a residential setting or in a person's own home. Your manager will have written risk assessments and behavioural guidelines for each individual who presents challenging behaviour and you must follow these. If you do not follow these, it could confuse the individual because you may respond one way and other staff may respond in a different way. You should avoid confusing the person, as doing so could put yourself and/or others in danger.

What is challenging behaviour?

Challenging behaviour is 'culturally abnormal behaviour of such intensity, frequency or duration that the person or others are likely to be placed in serious jeopardy or behaviour which is likely to seriously limit or delay access to and use of ordinary community facilities' (Emerson 1995, p.3).

✍ Discuss the above definition with your supervisor and see if it relates to the people you support.

. . . .

. . . .

. . . .

. . . .

Reasons why people challenge the service

There are many reasons why individuals challenge the service and here are a few examples:

- difficulty in communicating
- problems getting their message across
- frustration
- not being understood
- anger
- bereavement
- health issues
- boredom.

✍ Write here how you feel when you are bored:

....

....

....

....

....

✍ How do you think the individuals you are supporting feel when they are bored?

....

....

....

....

....

✍ What can be put in place to ensure the people you support do not have days when they are bored?

....

....

....

....

....

> Please remember that a structured day for the individuals can reduce challenging behaviour. This does not necessarily mean a structured day from the time the individual gets up to the time he or she goes to bed. Some people need structure for some of the day whereas others may need structure for most of the day or even the whole day.

How staff members can escalate a situation

There are many ways in which staff members can make matters worse, for example:

- miscommunicating or not understanding
- using an inappropriate tone of voice
- shouting at service users
- forcing instead of encouraging
- behaving inconsistently
- allowing personality clashes
- bickering with other staff members
- making unreasonable requests
- saying 'No' without an explanation
- using inappropriate body language
- ignoring the people they support
- having an unsympathetic attitude
- being in a bad mood.

For your own safety you should refrain from wearing the following items:

- Tight clothing: you need loose clothing to move your arms, shoulders, etc.
- Shoes with raised heels and/or open-toed shoes: wearing heels could prevent you from balancing and quickly moving from a situation should you need to.
- False nails, because these can scratch others and/or get caught on someone or something and be ripped off.

- Facial jewellery, jewellery around the neck and earrings other than studs, because these can catch on something or someone and you could be injured.

Dealing with challenging behaviour

> When someone presents with challenging behaviour, support him/her in a non-confrontational planned way. Follow the guidelines in the individual's care plan.

Remember the five stages of emotional arousal: triggering, build up, crisis, recovery and post-crisis depression.

1. *Triggering*: challenging behaviour is always caused by something and we call this a 'trigger'. The challenging behaviour can be triggered by various things, such as not being able to express oneself, or not being listened to, constantly not being thanked for doing things, something unpleasant that has happened in the past, being shouted or laughed at, being disrespected, ignored or undervalued, staff always doing things for the individual when the person can do things for himself, etc.

   What should I do?

   ° You need to monitor what is happening.

   ° Inform others.

2. *Build up*: you will notice changes in the person. The individual may become more agitated, or more active, become abusive and breathe heavily.

   What should I do?

   ° Approach in a careful manner.

   ° Try to understand the reasons why the individual is doing what he or she is doing.

   ° Respond and listen to what the service user is telling you.

   ° The situation should then be contained or defused.

3. *Crisis*: if the individual is still anxious then it may reach the crisis stage: the service user has become irrational and possibly lost control. You need to be thinking about yourself and others in the area. Try to reassure the

individual and follow any behavioural programmes or risk assessments that are written to support the individual.

What should I do?

- Follow the care plan or risk assessment.

- Look at ways to diffuse the situation.

- Maintain eye contact, but blink occasionally; *do not* stare. This shows concern for the service user, reinforcing that you are there for support and that you are not apprehensive.

- Use peripheral vision (vision from the corner of your eye) to check if anyone or anything is coming at you from the sides.

- See what is happening with the individual's hands and feet, check who else is entering the room and see if anyone else is in distress.

- Keep voice at a low level and in a calm tone. This shows concern rather than agitation, reinforcing that you are in control of the situation and preventing you from showing signs of agitation or apprehension.

- Try to understand why the person is anxious.

- Respond in a way that shows you are listening.

- Keep your facial expression neutral. This keeps you from showing any negative feelings and prevents your eye contact becoming a stare.

- Keep hands at waist height: this is non-confrontational, open to gestures and provides protection. You can then use your arms to block any blows that may come your way.

- Stand sideways on: this is non-confrontational and means you can move quickly from the area if needed.

4. *Recovery*: when the individual is beginning to relax we call this *recovery*.

   What should I do?

   - Offer reassurance and avoid the trigger that started the incident.

   - Avoid any other triggers.

   - Offer activities or opportunities that will change the person's frame of mind and make him or her feel better.

   - Explain that you value the person but you do not condone the behaviour.

5. *Post-crisis depression*: some service users may become withdrawn or feel low.

   What should I do?

   - Offer support, but do not try to change the individual's mood.

○ Offer activities that will help the individual to feel better.

○ The individual may appreciate some counselling, which can be an informal conversation with yourself or be arranged with a professional counsellor.

What to do after the incident

Each individual should have a chart to be completed when they have been anxious. This form is called an Antecedent, Behaviour, Consequences chart (for short, an ABC chart). By recording what happened prior to, during and after the event, you will be able to identify why the incident happened and put a plan in place to reduce the risk of it happening again.

The ABC chart enables you to record and monitor incidents involving the people you support. Along with the team you can discuss the information on the ABC chart and learn how to manage incidents like this if they occur again. Where possible, the service user should have the opportunity to reflect on what happened and why it happened.

 Reflecting on what happened could be a trigger for some individuals, so please discuss any incidents further with your manager.

The ABC chart will show you that you need to record:

• what the individual was doing before the incident (antecedent)

• details of the incident (behaviour)

• what the individual did after the incident (consequences).

If you complete this chart for a period of time, e.g. two weeks, you will see a pattern of what is upsetting the individual. This will then enable you to put something in place to prevent it happening again. An example of an ABC chart is shown next.

Name of individual: . . . . **Review date:**. . . . .

Date	Before the incident	Details of incident	What the individual did afterwards	Signature of staff

Ensure that you and others who witnessed the incident have an opportunity to talk through what happened.

Discuss the incident with your manager and reflect on what happened. Were there any learning points? Was there anything that you could have done differently? How can it be prevented from happening again? How do people feel prior to, during and after an incident?

. . . .

. . . .

. . . .

. . . .

. . . .

. . . .

Whether you are an individual receiving a service or a staff member, the reactions can be different for each person. Some people feel very anxious; others feel quite relaxed at the time and then become stressed after an event.

What we all have in common when reacting to a stressful event is the following:

- The adrenalin flows and the liver releases glucose to help muscles work effectively.

- Our breathing gets faster, which results in an increase in blood pressure.

- Churning stomach and dry mouth can happen as blood is diverted from the digestive system.

- Our muscles will tense.

- Our pupils widen to help us see more clearly.

- Once an incident has finished, the body should return to normal.

- If the incident has a long duration, the body will continue to do the above which could impact on one's health.

If at any time while supporting an incident you feel you need 'time out' (a break from the situation) discuss this as soon as is practicable with your senior or manager. It is a strength to do this and a period of 'time out' may be given when appropriate.

If after the event you are experiencing difficulty, such as stress or unease about working with specific individuals, please discuss it with your supervisor or manager. In the event of these two being off duty, you can discuss it with another senior member of staff, who will be happy to talk through the situation with you.

After each incident your company has a legal duty to review all relevant risk assessments relating to the person or people involved and the tasks involved in the incident. Your manager will show you the revised risk assessments that will contain revised measures to combat any future situation.

✍ What support would you like your manager to offer you? Please write your thoughts below. When reading this question you may feel that you do not need support, but everyone needs support.

. . . .

. . . .

. . . .

. . . .

. . . .

. . . .

The Government's National Task Force on Violence to Social Care Staff places a greater emphasis on support after a violent incident that results in physical or emotional harm to a staff member. Your organization must give prominence to the provision of debriefing, counselling and other forms of support. This can be done only if you inform people about what support suits you.

All of the following need to be in place:

- Making a structure for some or all of the day for the individual.

- Having an ABC chart to record behaviour.

- Ensuring there is sufficient staffing, e.g. working in twos if appropriate.

- Having a personal alarm (if appropriate).

- Possessing an ID card, which can be kept discreetly in your pocket and brought out if you are outside and one of the people you support is presenting challenging behaviour. If a member of the public is trying to get involved, show them the ID card and either ask the person to leave you alone or fetch a colleague or the police.

- Attending or receiving training on how to reduce or prevent challenging behaviour.

- Attending or receiving training on control and restraint if appropriate. Please note: you must not do any control and restraint unless there is an agreed procedure in place which has been agreed within a multidisciplinary team and you have received training.

After each incident:

- Complete the individual's ABC chart.

- Complete a Health and Safety incident form.

- Ask for time out if you need it.

- Discuss the incident with your manager, e.g.

  - talk through what happened

  - could you have done anything to prevent it happening?

  - did you follow the guidelines?

  - do the guidelines need to be reviewed and updated?

✍ Discuss with your supervisor the following questions:

Which individuals challenge? What are the risks involved to the individuals, yourself and/or others? (Please do not write any individuals' names here; for clarity, you could refer to the individuals as 'Ms A', 'Mr B' and so on.)

. . . .

. . . .

. . . .

. . . .

Where is the risk assessment?

. . . .

. . . .

What are the risks?

. . . .

. . . .

. . . .

. . . .

How can you maintain your own safety?

. . . .

. . . .

. . . .

. . . .

What triggers these behaviours and how can you prevent them?

. . . .

. . . .

. . . .

. . . .

When will you receive challenging behaviour training and control and restraint training (if appropriate)?

. . . .

. . . .

Who should you give the completed Health and Safety incident form to after you have recorded an incident? If the answer is the manager and it happens to be his or her day off, where should you store the form until he or she returns?

. . . .

. . . .

. . . .

. . . .

True and False Exercises

Try these 'true and false' exercises and check the answers with your manager or supervisor.

✍ Questions to test your knowledge

The fridge temperature can be between 1 and 9°C	True/False
The freezer temperature can be +18°C	True/False
The same cloth can be used in the kitchen and the bathroom	True/False
Only coloured plasters should be worn	True/False
Knees should be bent when moving an object	True/False
You must not use any manual handling equipment, give first aid or administer medication until you receive training	True/False
You should wash hands in hot water and use a pump soap	True/False
You should wear PPE at all times, including in the kitchen	True/False
It is important to report and record	True/False
Jewellery and false nails can be worn	True/False

✍ One of the people you support has told you that he would like to go to the shops by himself. What do you now need to do?

. . . .

. . . .

. . . .

. . . .

. . . .

Please discuss your answers with your manager or supervisor.

. . . .

. . . .

. . . .

. . . .

Self-Assessment Tool

✎ I now know:

What a risk assessment is	Yes/No
What a COSHH assessment is	Yes/No
What an accident, incident, near miss form is	Yes/No
How to protect the spine when moving or handling objects	Yes/No
The basic legislation that underpins moving and handling	Yes/No
My responsibility in identifying health and safety risks in the environment	Yes/No
What to do if electricity, gas or water need to be turned off in an emergency	Yes/No
The limits of my responsibility and ability in relation to emergency first aid	Yes/No
The fire extinguishers and their different purposes	Yes/No
What Personal Protective Equipment is	Yes/No
Where to find more information on policies and procedures	Yes/No
How to wash my hands thoroughly using the six steps to hand-washing	Yes/No

I am aware that I must attend the following training if I have not already done so:

First aid	Attended/Not attended
Risk assessment	Attended/Not attended
Basic food hygiene	Attended/Not attended
Medication	Attended/Not attended
Inanimate loads	Attended/Not attended
Manual handling (if applicable to your role)	Attended/Not attended
Challenging behaviour (if applicable to your role)	Attended/Not attended
Control and restraint (if applicable to your role)	Attended/Not attended

Signature of learner. . . . . Date. . . . .

Signature of supervisor . . . . Date. . . . .

What one thing will you do differently as a result of completing this training?

. . . .

. . . .

Certificate

. . . .

Name of company

THIS IS TO CERTIFY THAT

. . . .

Name of learner

Has completed training on

Health and Safety

ON

. . . .

Date

Name of Manager/Trainer . . . .

Signature of Manager/Trainer. . . . .

Name of workplace/training venue . . . .

Date . . . .

This training has covered:

- Roles and responsibilities
- Monitoring and maintaining a safe environment
- Legislation
- Infection control
- Health emergencies including electricity, fire, gas and water
- Challenging behaviour
- Security
- Lone working
- Recording and reporting

Knowledge Specification Chart

WHERE TO FIND THE KNOWLEDGE SPECIFICATION (KS) FOR NVQ UNIT 32

KS		Pages
1	Legal and organizational requirements on equality, diversity, discrimination and rights when working with individuals, key people and others when monitoring and promoting health and safety.	9, 13, 14, 15, 17, 28, 38, 45, 69
2	How to provide active support and promote individuals' rights, choice and well-being while promoting healthy and safe working practices and minimiszing risks from incidents and emergencies.	13, 17, 19, 38
3	Codes of practice and conduct; standards and guidance relevant to your own and others' roles, responsibilities, accountability and duties in relation to health, safety and when dealing with incidents and emergencies.	10, 13, 15, 17, 28, 35, 45, 51, 69, 81, 87
4	Current local, UK and European legislation and organisational requirements, procedures and practices for:	
	(a) data protection, including recording, reporting, storage, security and sharing of information	21, 25, 36, 38, 103
	(b) risk assessment and management	16, 28, 37, 41, 48, 71, 76, 96
	(c) the protection of yourself, individuals, key people and others from danger, harm and abuse	17, 35, 45, 46, 51, 71, 73
	(d) monitoring and maintaining health, safety and security in the workplace	28, 29, 45, 48, 51, 60, 71
	(e) dealing with incidents and emergencies	21, 79, 89, 91

5	The purpose of, and arrangements for supervision when involved in incidents and emergencies.	94
6	How and where to access information and support that can inform your practice on health, safety and dealing with incidents and emergencies.	9, 13, 14, 38, 79, 103
7	The effects of stress and distress on yourself, individuals, key people and others.	74, 106
8	Conditions and issues you are likely to face in your work with individuals and key people.	35, 95, 97, 99, 101, 109
9	Methods of supporting individuals to: (a) express their needs and preferences (b) understand and take responsibility for promoting their own health and care (c) assess and manage risks to their health and well-being.	14, 19, 38, 95
10	How to work with, and resolve conflicts that you are likely to meet.	13, 38, 95, 97
11	Methods of: (a) monitoring activities and the environment to minimize risk and keep the environment free from hazards (b) storing different equipment and materials safely and securely (c) minimizing the risk of contamination and infection.	28, 31, 35, 38, 97 32, 45 46, 51, 55
12	How to deal and work with hazardous and non-hazardous materials, equipment and waste, in order to minimize the risks of contamination and danger to yourself, individuals, key people and others with whom you work and are responsible for.	35, 45, 46, 51, 97
13	Procedures, techniques and the differing types of equipment to enable you to lift, move and handle people, materials and items safely.	69
14	How to assess risks to yourself, individuals, key people and others.	37, 41, 57, 71, 76, 78

15	The type of security and health incidents and emergencies that might happen in your area of work and working environment.	79, 95, 96, 97
16	The appropriate action to take for different security and health incidents and emergencies.	79, 93, 96, 97
17	Your own capabilities to deal with an accident and emergency, and when and how to summon additional help.	79
18	How to promote health and safety to others, including the modelling of good practice.	13, 46, 51, 60

References and Further Reading

REFERENCES

Department of Health (2000) *Domiciliary Care: National Minimum Standards* (Commission for Social Care Inspection Communication Standard). London: Stationery Office. Available at www.dh.gov.uk/prod_consum_dh/groups/dh_digitalassets/@dh/@en/documents/digitalasset/dh_4018671.pdf, accessed on 19 October 2008.

Department of Health (2003) *Care Homes for Adults (18–65)* (Commission for Social Care Inspection Communication Standard). London: Stationery Office. Available at www.csci.org.uk/professional/care_providers/all_services/national_minimum_standards.aspx, accessed on 19 October 2008.

Emerson, E. (1995) *Challenging Behaviour: Analysis and Intervention in People With Learning Difficulties.* Cambridge: Cambridge University Press.

General Social Care Council (GSCC) (2002) *Codes of Practice.* London: GSCC. Available at www.gscc.org.uk/codes, accessed on 19 October 2008.

Government's National Task Force on Violence to Social Care Staff. www.dh.gov.uk/en/Managingyourorganisation/Humanresourcesandtraining/NationalTaskForceonViolence/index.htm, accessed 19 May 2009.

Health and Safety Commission (2008) *A Strategy for Workplace Health and Safety in Great Britain to 2010 and Beyond.* London: Health and Safety Executive. Available at www.hse.gov.uk/consult/condocs/strategycd.pdf, accessed on 15 December 2008.

Health and Safety Executive (HSE) (1997) *Successful Health and Safety Management,* HSG65. London: HSE Books.

Health and Safety Executive (HSE) (2008) *Stress-Related and Psychological Disorders.* London: HSE. Available at www.hse.gov.uk/statistics/causdis/stress/index.htm, accessed on 15 December 2008.

FURTHER READING

Department of Health (2007) *Emergency Planning.* London: DoH. Available at www.dh.gov.uk/en/Managingyourorganisation/Emergencyplanning/index.htm, accessed on 15 December 2008.

Hartropp, H. (2006) *Hygiene in Health and Social Care.* London: Chartered Institute of Environmental Health.

Homer, J.M. (1993) *Workplace Environment, Health and Safety Management: A Practical Guide* London: Chartered Institute of Environmental Health.

Legislation and Useful Websites

LEGISLATION THAT COULD BE APPLICABLE TO THE PEOPLE YOU SUPPORT

Access to Health Records Act 1990

This Act informs us that individuals can have access to their medical records and that no one, including family, can see these records without the individual's permission.

Care Standards Act 2000

The Care Standards Act 2000 (CSA) provides for the administration of a variety of care institutions, including children's homes, independent hospitals, nursing home and residential care homes.

Data Protection Act 1998

This Act protects the rights of the individual on information that is obtained, stored, processed or supplied and applies to both computerized and paper records and requires that appropriate security measures are in place.

Health and Safety at Work Act 1974

This Act promotes the security and health, safety and welfare of people at work and this also includes individuals who you support.

Human Rights Act 2000

This Act promotes the fundamental rights and freedoms contained in the European Convention on Human Rights.

Mental Capacity Act 2005

This Act provides a clearer legal framework for people who lack capacity and sets out key principles and safeguards. It also includes the 'Deprivation of liberty safeguards' which aims to provide legal protection for vulnerable people who are deprived of their liberty other than under the Mental Health Act 1983. This act came into effect in April 2009.

Mental Health Act 1983

This Act regulates the treatment of mentally ill people.

NHS and Community Care Act 1990

This Act helps people live safely in the community.

Safeguarding Vulnerable Groups Act 2006

This aim of this Act is to strengthen current safeguarding arrangements and prevent unsuitable people from working with children and adults who are vulnerable. It will change the way vetting happens and will now be introduced in July 2010.

USEFUL WEBSITES

All the following websites were accessed on 15 December 2008.

Age Concern

www.ageconcern.org.uk
Promotes the well-being of all older people.

AID Training and Operations Ltd

www.aid-training.co.uk
Delivers first aid and health and safety training throughout the UK.

Alzheimer's Society

www.alzheimers.org.uk
This is the leading UK care and research charity for people with dementia, their families and carers.

Care Quality Commission

www.cqc.org.uk
CQC inspect and report on care services and councils. They are independent but set up by government to improve social care and stamp out bad practice.

Communication Matters

www.communicationmatters.org.uk
National voluntary organisation of members concerned with augmentative and alternative communications.

Department of Health

www.dh.gov.uk
Providing health and social care policy, guidance and publications for NHS and social care professionals.

General Social Care Council

www.gscc.org.uk

Sets standards of conduct and practice for social care workers and their employers in England.

Health and Safety Executive

www.hse.gov.uk

HSE's job is to protect people against risks to health or safety arising out of work activities. Provides advice, guidance, regulations and inspections.

Livability

www.livability.org.uk

Providing choices for disabled people.

Mencap

www.mencap.org.uk

Mencap is the voice of learning disability and works with people with a learning disability to change laws and services, challenge prejudice and directly support thousands of people with a learning disability to live their lives as they choose.

Mind

www.mind.org.uk

Mind is the leading mental health charity in England and Wales. We work to create a better life for everyone with experience of mental distress.

National Institute for Health and Clinical Excellence

www.nice.org.uk

NICE is an independent organisation responsible for providing national guidance on promoting good health and preventing and treating ill health.

The National Resource for Infection Control (NRIC)

www.nric.org.uk

NRIC is a project developed by healthcare professionals, aimed at being a single-access point to existing resources within infection control for both Infection Control and all other healthcare staff.

Respect

www.respect.uk.net

Respect is the UK membership association for domestic violence perpetrator programmes and associated support services. The key focus is on increasing the safety of those experiencing domestic violence through promoting effective interventions with perpetrators.

Respond

www.respond.org.uk

Respond provides a range of services to both victims and perpetrators of sexual abuse who have learning disabilities and those who have been affected by other trauma. The services extend to support and training for families, carers and professionals.

RIDDOR (Reporting of Injuries, Diseases and Dangerous Occurrences Regulations 1995)

www.hse.gov.uk/riddor

These regulations place a legal duty on employers, self-employed people and people in control of premises to report work-related deaths, major injuries or over-three-day injuries, work related diseases, and dangerous occurrences (near miss accidents).

Royal National Institute for Deaf People

www.RNID.org.uk

Changing the world for deaf and hard of hearing people. RNID is the largest charity representing the nine million deaf and hard of hearing people in the UK.

Royal National Institute of Blind People

www.RNIB.org.uk

National UK charity providing a good range of information for blind or partially sighted people.

Scope

www.scope.org.uk

Scope is a UK disability organization whose focus is people with cerebral palsy.

United Response

www.unitedresponse.org.uk

United Response supports people with learning disabilities, mental health needs or physical disabilities to live in the community, across England and in Wales.

Valuing People

http://valuingpeople.gov.uk

Valuing People is the government's plan for making the lives of people with learning disabilities and the lives of their families better.

Voice UK

www.voiceuk.org.uk

A national charity supporting people with learning disabilities and other vulnerable people who have experienced crime or abuse.